And Then I Met Margaret

Peter

You're great

Rob White

And Then I Met Margaret

STORIES OF
ORDINARY GURUS
I'VE MET

Rob White

Mind Adventure Press
Boston, MA

Published by
Mind Adventure Press
Boston, MA

ISBN 978-0-9802299-6-7

Versions of some stories in this book originally appeared in
The Huffington Post.

Cover and text by Mayapriya Long, Bookwrights.com

To my sister Buffy, who gave many of my childhood moments a touch of magic with a single wave of her Cinderella wand. Although she's no longer physically here, her magic remains within me.

CONTENTS

INTRODUCTION: Gurus in Our Midst 1

CHAPTER 1: The Queen of Hearts 7

CHAPTER 2: Pebbles and Fool's Gold 15

CHAPTER 3: The Great Vitim's Candy Caper 21

CHAPTER 4: Toeing the Line 27

CHAPTER 5: Standing Firm on Thin Ice 35

CHAPTER 6: Fitting In 43

CHAPTER 7: Shakespeare in My Left Pants Pocket 55

CHAPTER 8: A Little Trick I Like to Call "Pay Attention" 65

CHAPTER 9: Craving a Lilac Mint 73

CHAPTER 10: I Decided I Was Smarter than I Thought I Was 79

CHAPTER 11: The $50K Lie 93

CHAPTER 12: The $3M Shakeup 103

CHAPTER 13: Flying Dangerously 113

CHAPTER 14: Life in the Fast Lane 121

CHAPTER 15: Running with the Bulls 129

CHAPTER 16: It's Just Me 137

CHAPTER 17: The Squawk Heard Round the World 147

CHAPTER 18: The Guru in the Red Dress 155

CHAPTER 19: The Maasai Mother 163

CHAPTER 20: License and Registration, Please 171

CHAPTER 21: I Decided Not to Die 177

EPILOGUE 183

ACKNOWLEDGMENTS 185

ABOUT THE AUTHOR 187

INTRODUCTION

Gurus in Our Midst

Some people say that I've been pretty darn lucky all of my life. I believe luck isn't something that happens to me; luck is something that happens *through* me. Let me explain.

I hail from a poor town and grew up with a model of reality that said scrambling for money is the way it shall be. But then I surprised everyone, including myself, and became very good at making money. The moment I stopped thinking that "success is possible, but not probable," I became a better judge of what decisions and choices were best for me. I began redirecting my life path from being a kid born in a mill town, destined to work in a local factory, to being a big-city schoolteacher. From there, I became a highly successful real estate entrepreneur and restaurateur on both the East and West coasts. But in spite of these wins, I felt like there was still something lacking. I'd convinced myself that bigger homes, fancier cars, and luxury cruises to exotic ports would give me inner satisfaction. To the contrary, these acquisitions and junkets only intensified the feeling that something was missing. My exterior world reflected material wealth, but my interior world was spiritually bankrupt.

I was around age fifty when I decided to direct my money and time toward a new purpose. I set out in search of gurus who could share their wisdom and help me feel as rich on the inside as I appeared on the outside. My quest took me to Los Angeles, Miami, Denver, New York, San Francisco, Atlanta, Chicago, New Orleans, San Diego, Washington DC, Baltimore, San Jose, Greensboro, Austin, Hartford, and Honolulu. I traveled as far as Africa to observe how people, unaffected by the industrialized world, experience a deep inner sense of lasting peace and happiness. I logged more than 400,000 frequent flyer miles and spent a small fortune attending speeches, seminars, workshops, retreats, symposia, conventions, fire-walking rituals, and sweat lodge powwows. I met great thinkers on subjects ranging from reclaiming your personal power and eradicating self-contradictions to overcoming self-doubt and realizing divine things more beautiful than words can describe.

I attended EST and met with the founder Werner Erhard. Werner taught me to look beyond the self-descriptive identity that exists at the level of language.

I hung out with Alan Watts, philosopher and author of *The Way of Zen*. One afternoon on his houseboat in Sausalito, Alan taught me that inner illumination must come first before you'll ever understand your outer life.

I met with Stephan Covey, author of the classic *7 Habits* books, who taught me that we enhance our chances of success by programming the mind to stop arguing with itself.

I spent two weeks on a retreat with Ram Dass, spiritual teacher and author of *Be Here Now*. Ram Dass taught me that there is a power in me right now that is waiting to release into creative action.

I met Marianne Williamson at a weekend spiritual retreat, an internationally renowned lecturer and author of the bestseller, *A Return to Love:* Marianne taught me that an unwanted life is unnecessary when you live with love in your heart.

I attended a brown-bag lunch seminar given by W. Clemente Stone, a rags-to-riches poster child who founded and ran a billion-dollar insurance company. I learned from Mr. Stone that the path to success begins when you take a new internal direction.

I met with Jim Rohn, author of *The Art of Exceptional Living*, and known for his many incredibly insightful quotes. He was an early teacher to Tony Robbins, and a mentor to thousands. Jim taught me that my inherent successful nature awaits my release, which can only happen through my active awareness of it.

I met with motivational speaker Tony Robbins and attended several of his seminars and workshops. Tony taught me ways to transform my mind from being a noisy boss to a loyal servant. At one point, when I had cold feet, I decided to take Tolly Burkan's Fire Walk Certification Course. If it was good enough for Tony, it was good enough for me.

I attended a seminar by W. Edwards Deming, who revolutionized our thinking about process and efficiency and transformed the manufacturing world. Edward taught me that when you settle for nothing less than excellence, you become part of a rare species that's in huge demand.

I participated in a "Born to Win" seminar with Zig Ziglar, and later had dinner with him. Zig pointed out that once you stop ordinary thoughts from reigning in your mind, extraordinary thinking can begin.

I attended a workshop lead by Deepak Chopra, holistic health expert and best-selling author. Deepak taught me that being in the right place is a matter of being in *your* right place.

I conferred with Louise Hay, author of the smash hit, *You Can Heal Your Life*, and founder of Hay House, publisher of numerous best-selling self-help books. Louise spoke of the importance of always thinking of ourselves in terms of potential.

I spoke with Brian Tracy, the popular motivational speaker and author of the big seller, *Eat That Frog*. Brian taught me that by desiring a new life, I've already made a great start in the right direction.

I spent hours, one weekend, chatting with Og Mandino, author of the fifty-million-copy bestseller, *The Greatest Salesman in the World*. I truly loved my chats with Og. He taught me that if there's any magic genie in a bottle, it's the magic that is "bottled up" deep inside each of us.

I spoke with John Grinder, cofounder of NLP and author of many books on the subject. He made it clear that we are all infinitely more resourceful than we think; and in every moment, we do the best we can with the resources we have available. The key to happiness and success is to learn how to put ourselves in a resourceful state.

I met at least a dozen other great thinkers who all pointed to the fact that there is a wondrous, creative power at the center of each of us, and that most of us accomplish only a fraction of what we're capable of achieving.

And then . . . I met Margaret, a grade school student who awakened me to the possibility of starting a new life, as a new person, with a single simple question . . . I met a Maasai mother who demonstrated that when we are willing to go beyond ourselves, there are no boundaries to what we can do . . . I met Debbie, a middle school student, who taught me that if we're to do something strikingly new, we must be willing to think something strikingly new about ourselves . . . I met fifteen thousand people, who, with the clap of thirty thousand hands, helped me see the richness of authenticity . . . and I met Peter, a former peanut vendor who turned medical wisdom on its head by simply deciding that he wasn't going to die.

In the following pages, you'll meet these and other "unexpected gurus" who offered me opportunities to understand myself and life correctly. Life is constantly offering us opportunities to meet these gurus. Though they may not consciously know it, their purpose is to help us shatter self-limiting myths that prevent us from fully experiencing our lives.

These gurus provide "transformational moments" by helping us destroy those myths we hold about ourselves. At the core of these myths are lies that stop us from having inspiring insights that enable us to re-evaluate ourselves and our potential. These lies also prevent us from gaining a deeper understanding of humanity and blind us to important life lessons.

The moment of transformation doesn't always happen immediately, even though the process of change has begun. As you'll see in my stories, the moment may come *decades* later! Regardless of how long it takes for change to happen, the transformation is ultimately dependent upon our denying a lie that has been stopping us from breaking through to higher levels of living. The joy of revealing an "untruth" is the awakening moment when you expand your awareness of things as they truly are.

But it's important to understand that the act of deconstructing a myth is more than just revealing an untruth and having an insight—there must also be an equal and opposite reaction to the myth. That is, you must go out in the world and act as though your newly discovered truth is so. You must give the same energy to the truth that you gave to the myth. You'll see how I did this as you read my stories.

As I enter my seventh decade on this planet, I accept that I will never know everything that lies ahead on the next part of my journey. But I do know this: if I look at my life through the lens of transformational opportunities, I open my eyes and my heart to life's unexpected teachers. And these gurus always show up at the perfect time and right place to disrupt an old pattern of thinking. In such positively disruptive moments, it's becoming easier and easier for me to see the next forward step I should take.

In Chapter 12, you'll meet Margaret, the youngest and most influential of the unexpected gurus in my life. Margaret truly upset my mental applecart by helping me to see my distorted view of reality, and how I placed myself smack-dab in the middle of it. Since then, Margaret's positive impact has been ongoing. That's why I named this entire collection of stories after her. I bet there's a Margaret in your life, too—you need only open your eyes and heart, and your unexpected guru will appear.

Your happiness, your success, your unique self-expression and your feeling of inner satisfaction all begins with you. But it often takes an unassuming teacher or event to awaken you to that possibility and offer the insight you need to upgrade it from possible to probable—to downright inevitable.

Are you ready?

CHAPTER 1

The Queen of Hearts

—◆—

The myth I believed:

Kindness is an act of self-interest.

E very small town has its own set of unwritten rules that reflect the fabric of its culture, its code of honor, its values and mores, and its expectations for future generations. In the mill town where I grew up, one of the unwritten rules was that young men would best serve themselves, their family, and the community if they worked hard to graduate from high school and then worked in one of two mills. And the young women would serve best if they married, had children, and tended to the household.

Women who didn't marry were called "old maids" and became the target of gossip and occasional insults. These women were often shy and stayed home because they didn't fit in. In effect, they underwent voluntary house arrest, creating a cycle that ensured that they'd remain alone.

My family unerringly followed the formal rules of the law and the unwritten rules of the town, with one exception: Aunt Theresa. She had the ill fortune of aging into her thirties unattached. To make matters worse, she was tall and, at first glance, lacked those feminine features accepted by society's standards. Nonetheless, she was my aunt, and I loved when she'd come over to visit. She lived a few streets away and frequently came by bearing freshly baked chocolate cupcakes with white frosting. These were the ambrosia of my youth, moist and delicious treats, unlike anything you could buy at the grocery store.

Aunt Theresa's visits were always exciting for me, and not just because of the delicious cupcakes. Here was an adult who enjoyed playing cards with me and my sisters at the kitchen table, sometimes for a whole hour!

Ironically, we played Old Maid, which was my favorite game, because it happened to be the only card game I understood at the age of five. Best of all, Aunt Theresa always brought a new deck of cards when she came to play Old Maid. I loved opening the new deck and shuffling them before we started playing. And she always gave me that duty.

The point of the game is that whoever is left with the dreaded Old Maid card, which bore an image of a haggard old witchlike woman, loses the game. I was a sensitive child, and I hated to lose. I was further upset when my two sisters would laugh and point, saying, "You're the old maid, Bobby. Ha, ha, old maid, old maid, old maid!"

Even though I had no idea what "Old Maid" meant, I knew it was bad. I'd inevitably begin pouting and run out of the room, refusing to play another round. I could sulk for an entire day after losing a hand.

Strangely, after several pouting sessions, while playing Old Maid with Aunt Theresa, my luck did a complete turnaround. For some reason, Aunt Theresa always ended up choosing the Old Maid card from my hand when it was just the two of us left in the game. I couldn't believe that she never caught on to my ingenious strategy of sliding the Old Maid card higher than the other card I had in my hand. She always took the bait! When the game was over, I'd laugh and say, "Aunt Theresa, you're the Old Maid!" I'd sometimes say it a dozen times, after which Aunt Theresa always smiled and said, "Darn it, Bobby, you tricked me again!"

As I grew into my teens, I got busy with my life, I saw less and less of Aunt Theresa. By the time I was in high school, I saw her very little. A year after graduating from college, my mother told me that Aunt Theresa was dying of a liver condition and I should come visit her. It was close to Valentine's Day, so I went to the hospital with a bright bouquet of flowers. She smiled as I placed them on the table by her bed. Although she was weak and frail, she brightly reminisced about the times we spent together when I was a young child. She said she especially treasured the card games at our kitchen table.

Aunt Theresa asked me to hand her the large cloth bag on the floor next to her bed. She reached in and explained that it was filled with keepsakes she saved over her lifetime, things that meant the most to her. Among the mementos was a small stack of cards bound by a rubber band. "I want you to have these, Bobby," she said.

As I turned over each card, I was amazed to see that they were Old Maid cards, just like the ones from the card decks we used years ago! Aunt Theresa laughed and said they were not just *like* the cards, they *were* the cards! She then confessed that she intentionally chose the Old Maid card from my hand because she knew how much the taunts of my sisters bothered me. As she spoke, my senses were overwhelmed with the heavenly scent of the chocolate cupcakes. The wondrous associations threw me back to my childhood; and once again, I felt her love for me, just like I felt it during those marvelous card games in the kitchen.

Aunt Theresa grew tired, and I knew it was time to go. "Bobby, save these cards, and remember the good times we had together, okay?" she asked.

I nodded, kissed her on the forehead, and said, "I'll see you soon, Aunt Theresa."

She died two days later.

After Aunt Theresa's funeral, I told my mother about the Old Maid cards. Her eyes grew teary, and she told me a sad story. Aunt Theresa actually came within a hair of escaping from old maid purgatory. When she was thirty-four, one of the workers at the mill, Brad, started courting her. No one knew about their relationship. Six months later, Brad decided he was ready to pop the big question. It was a tradition in our town that before you got down on your knees in front of your soon-to-be better half, you plunked yourself down on a bar stool at the Silver Spoon Cafe. You then raised your hand and displayed the engagement ring, at which point your bar buddies passed it around and continually roasted and toasted you for the big move you were making. This went on until everyone was ready to pass out. It was an instant, high octane stag party.

The night Brad held up the ring he'd purchased to pop the question, and announced his bride-to-be's name, the place was so quiet that you could hear an Old Maid card drop. One by one, Brad's drinking buddies chimed in, "Are you crazy?"

"She's over the hill."

"Have you had your glasses checked lately?"

"What's wrong with you?"

I know the Silver Spoon Café fiasco to be true; because a neighbor, who was bartending that night, told my mother the details. Within a few minutes, Brad realized the folly of his ways and announced that the wedding was off. The next day, he told Theresa about the change in plans. After that, she became reclusive and rarely went out of the house.

Against this backdrop, my mother's next revelation was even more startling—whenever Aunt Theresa "lost" a game with me, she removed the Old Maid card from the deck and added it to her collection. She'd then go out and buy a new box of cards, knowing I loved opening the new deck, so we could play again. These treks to buy new decks of Old Maid cards were some of the few times she left the house to walk down Main Street and visit W. T. Grant's twenty-five-cent store, located at the other end of the town. Although she'd become introverted, Theresa faithfully made the journey to delight me with new cards. I guess that's what a true queen of hearts does for someone she loves.

When I learned about Aunt Theresa's forays to the store, I realized how courageous she had been to endure the pain of being laughed at and called an "old maid" by me and my sisters—just to protect me from getting so upset when I lost. I felt a new kind of sadness for the loss of my aunt. I vowed to myself that I would not let Aunt Theresa's loving generosity die with me. I would pass along the precious lesson she taught me: there are some beautiful people in this world who do beautiful things for others, even though they may suffer greatly because they don't conform to the norm.

My chance to continue Aunt Theresa's generosity came as unexpectedly as the lesson she imparted to me. I had moved to Boston right before Aunt Theresa died. I'd taken a temporary job stocking shelves at a grocery store, figuring that I'd apply for a teaching position in the fall. The store manager, Roger, hired me, knowing that I was overqualified and probably wouldn't stay long; but he needed shelving clerks, and no one else was applying for the job.

During the first day at work, I met Gary, who'd been with the store for nearly a year. Gary was in his late twenties and was honest and hardworking, but he constantly made foolish mistakes. He put the cat food on the same shelf with the tuna cans one day; and the very next day, he put the ice cream with the milk where it soon thawed and made a big mess. You might assume he had a brain-part missing until you spoke with him. He was actually quite intelligent; his problem was that he didn't take the time to focus his mind on the activity at hand. He was much more interested in talking about the last Red Sox games—who played well or who made a grave error.

The more distracted Gary became, the more mistakes he made. One time he lost the keys to the store's back door, and the lock had to be changed. On the very same day, he spilled a gallon of olive oil on the aisle floor. "One more mistake, and you're done," Roger yelled in frustration.

Well, it wasn't long before a serious mistake occurred—he stamped forty egg cartons well below the retail price. Word about the "egg sale" traveled quickly, and there was a run on eggs at the store. Even after management caught the error and had the egg cartons stamped correctly, customers kept arguing with the cashiers that they had the right to purchase the eggs at ninety percent off.

At the end of the shift, the employees were all called together. Roger wanted to get to the bottom of the matter, and make an example of Gary. We all knew that when Gary was found responsible, he'd be fired; so, before the inquiry went too deep, I spoke up and said I'd put the wrong price-roll on the labeler. I added that I asked Gary to stamp the egg cartons because a delivery truck of bread had come in, and I had to set it up. I knew Gary wouldn't remember how the whole matter went down; he'd only remember that he did the stamping while rambling on about the Red Sox game the night before.

"Accurate pricing is vital," Roger exclaimed. "There's no room for error. This kind of mistake can put us out of business, and everyone loses their jobs." He announced that I was going to be let go because of my negligence.

While everyone else quietly filed out the door, Roger called me aside. He told me he knew that I had nothing to do with the matter, and that it was very kind of me to take the fall. Gary really couldn't afford to lose his job, especially since his prospects of getting another were slim. Roger went on to say that he was going to sit Gary down and tell him that he knew I took the blame for his error. He hoped Gary would appreciate what I'd done. More importantly, he hoped Gary learned a valuable lesson from the incident. Because, if he didn't—he was next to go.

Roger also told me that this was a "blessing in disguise" for me, because it was time for me to take action and land a teaching job. "Instead of showing up for work tomorrow, show your head in the school department. Here's a tip: sign up for substitute teaching."

He explained that his brother was a principal in one of the city's schools, and his brother had said numerous times that when a good substitute teacher comes along, a principal can request that the substitute be made permanent when the next vacancy comes. "If that happens, Bob, you'll go straight to the top of the list of qualified college graduates waiting to be chosen for teaching jobs."

That sounded like a great tip. The next day, I applied for a substitute teaching position. On the first day of school, I was called to take a temporary teaching position for a teacher who had suddenly become ill. I worked hard and volunteered to do "after school tutoring." When the teacher I was subbing for decided to take the year off—which was a stroke of luck for me—the principal made a call on my behalf. Just as Roger's brother predicted, I was placed at the top of the list and offered the permanent position.

What I hadn't shared with Roger was that my taking the blame for Gary's mistake was my way of honoring my Aunt Theresa. I was deliberately choosing the Old Maid card, so to speak. I'm certain she would have done the same thing had she been in my shoes.

We all possess the power of compassion that my aunt displayed. When we unleash that power by acting kindly, life always reciprocates in beautiful ways—ways we often cannot imagine.

The myth I believed:

Kindness is an act of self-interest.

The reality I discovered:

Kind acts demonstrate the height of love.

CHAPTER 2

Pebbles and Fool's Gold

—◈—

The myth I believed:

Magic happens randomly to me.

Everyone should have an Uncle Fred while growing up. I loved it when Uncle Fred came around to visit. I was proud of his success. He managed the local shoe store, and the spiffy new wingtips he wore said it all. They were always polished. Uncle Fred would say, "You can see your reflection in them; go ahead, take a look." With a pair of shoes like that, you ruled the world.

Shiny footwear aside, my parents got a big kick out of Uncle Fred, and bragged about how ambitious he was. My dad said that Uncle Fred was such a good salesman that he could sell refrigerators to Eskimos. Even though I heard that statement a thousand times, I still thought it was a hoot!

The incredible warmth and charm that Uncle Fred exuded made me feel good, no matter what mood I was in before he showed up. And his big, bright, ear-to-ear smile melted the hearts of all the women in town (another of my dad's favorite statements).

Best of all, Uncle Fred was a great storyteller and a first-class magician. He was not the run-of-the-mill kind of magician who could find a quarter in your ear—that was kid's stuff. Uncle Fred performed *real* magic.

One day, when I was about five, Uncle Fred stopped by to demonstrate an unbelievable act of sorcery. It's a good thing my best friend, Stevie Brown, happened to be hanging out with me on my grandmother's porch and was there to witness the amazing feat. Otherwise, no one would believe it had actually happened.

Stevie and I sat down on the front floor, while Uncle Fred proceeded to tell us that we were in for the magic trick of the century. He slowly searched the ground in front of the porch steps until he found the perfect pebble. Then he crouched down and pointed to the small rock in his palm. After letting us examine the pebble so we could verify it was just plain sidewalk stuff, Uncle Fred pulled out a fancy silk handkerchief (another sign of his success) from his back pants pocket. Uncle Fred shook the handkerchief open and carefully placed it over the palm of his hand, covering the pebble. He uttered the following incantation: "Abracadabra, puddin' pie, kiss the girls and make them cry."

Uncle Fred waited a second or two, and then whipped the handkerchief off his palm. To our sheer amazement, the pebble was gone. In its place sat a gleaming gold pirate's coin. We knew the coin was real, because it had a pirate's face on one side and a ship flying the Jolly Roger flag on the other.

Uncle Fred let us pick up the coin and flip it over and stare in awe; then he said to me, "Would you like to try this trick?"

"Oh, yeah!" I said, hardly able to contain my excitement.

Uncle Fred jumped down the steps and found another pebble suitable for transforming into gold. "Okay, let me have your hand." I extended my hand and Uncle Fred dropped the pebble into my palm. "You know what to do, Bobby. Here's the handkerchief. Place it over the pebble, then grab the corner and say, 'Abracadabra, puddin' pie, kiss the girls and make them cry,' and then snap the handkerchief off your palm!"

I was about to perform some serious magic when Uncle Fred said, "Oops, wait a minute. One more thing, Bobby . . . when you do this magic trick, never *ever* think about a black cat. They bring bad luck. If you think of a black cat, the magic won't happen."

"Okay, I won't think about a black cat," I promised.

Uncle Fred nodded and winked at me, signaling I was on my own.

I steeled myself, focused, and uttered the phrase, "Abracadabra puddin' pie, kiss the girls and make them cry." I then snapped off the handkerchief just as Uncle Fred had told me to do. I couldn't believe my eyes: no gold coin, just one gritty old pebble.

My disappointment was palpable. Uncle Fred put his hand on my shoulder and asked, "Bobby, did you think about a black cat?"

"I did, Uncle Fred. I couldn't help myself."

"That's okay," Uncle Fred said as he patted my shoulder. "It takes practice. You'll get it over time. Does your friend Stevie want to try it?"

Stevie's eyes grew wide. "Oh, yeah, I know I can do it."

Uncle Fred carefully explained the ritual again and warned Stevie about the perils of the black cat. Again, he nodded and winked, and then it was Stevie's turn.

"Don't worry, I'm not going to think of a black cat!" Stevie assured Uncle Fred, "I never think about black cats." Stevie then intoned, "Abracadabra, puddin' pie, kiss the girls and make them cry" as he whipped the handkerchief off his palm.

"It's the pebble! Rats! I *was* thinking about a black cat."

I nodded my head in solidarity and said, "Wow, it's hard *not* to think of a black cat, huh?"

After Uncle Fred left, Stevie and I went over the details of the magic we'd just experienced. We agreed that no one, anywhere, could have better shoes than Uncle Fred's. We agreed that Uncle Fred was the only person we knew who carried a nice silk handkerchief in his back pocket. Best of all, we agreed that Uncle Fred was the only guy in the whole wide world who could do the magic trick without *once* thinking of a black cat. He was our hero.

This transformational opportunity took two decades to ripen for me. Twenty years later, I was deeply entrenched in my teaching career. Along with imparting academic content, I tried to weave in a bit of positive life philosophy. This was the time in my life when I was gobbling up literature about the power of positive thinking, and I enjoyed sharing the lessons I was learning. I felt this was especially important for those students with low expectations about what life had in store for them.

I often told my students that they needed to stop looking at the negative side of things if they wanted their dreams to come true. "A happy, successful life comes with the right thoughts and the right feelings," I explained. When they began complaining and blamed the world for all their problems, I told them to flip the coin over; there's always a bright side.

One day, in the midst of telling one of my inspirational stories, it dawned on me that I was following my Uncle Fred's footsteps. I was teaching my students the same lesson Uncle Fred taught me through the pebble and coin trick: If a black cat prowls around in your mind, it will stop you from seeing the golden opportunities right in front of you. It will blind you to the good things that life continually offers you.

After this realization, I was so excited that I told one of my classes about Uncle Fred and the pebble and pirate coin story from my youth. Most of the students laughed. A few commented on what a dopey kid I must have been to believe that a rock could turn into a gold coin. I wasn't deterred. I explained that Uncle Fred was one of my childhood heroes because of his great attitude; and, if they wanted to spiral their own attitudes upward, they ought to spend more time mining for golden opportunities than whining about black cats crossing their paths.

Over the next few weeks, I challenged them to find any black cats that might be lurking in their heads—things that dragged them down when they thought about finding golden opportunities in the world and achieving their dreams. Out of this class discussion came a class chant. Whenever a student complained about how hard the homework was or how unfair a teacher could be, the other students chanted, "Start mining, stop whining."

This chant led to some great classroom conversations and, I'd like to think, even better grades, and a more fantastic life in the coming years.

The myth I believed:

Magic happens randomly to me.

The reality I discovered:

Magic deliberately happens because of me.

CHAPTER 3

The Great Vitim's Candy Caper

—◈—

The myth I believed:

**There's no harm to acting with
a personal angle in mind.**

W here I grew up, the favorite afternoon activity was a trip to Vitim's corner store. Who could resist its lure, what with the abundant supply of candy, snack food, and sugary beverages that adorned the shelves. The essential one-stop, afterschool stop, Vitim's could have been a set from *Pleasantville* or the subject of a Norman Rockwell painting. Occasionally, you'd even spot a character who looked like "the Fonz" from *Happy Days,* picking up his pack of butts before jumping on a motorcycle and roaring off down the street.

One of the biggest draws for us was a bowl of hard sucking-candies by the cash register. If you took a candy, you dropped a penny in the tin next to the bowl. *One candy out, one penny in*. Life was simple.

One day, I went in the store and saw old man Vitim restocking a shelf, so I knew that I was on the honor system with regard to the "candy out, penny in" ritual. I always played by the rules; although I noticed that my buddy, Dennis, sometimes cheated by taking two candies out and putting only one penny in. On this occasion, I reached into my pocket and found myself penniless. So I slipped over to the dark side, popping a candy into my mouth and rattling the penny bowl so it sounded like I'd just added a coin. *One candy out, no penny in*. Life was getting complicated.

My heart pounded at the thought of getting away with my first grand theft. But then guilt crept in, followed by terror, as I realized that the customer in back of me, an old guy, probably in his forties, had witnessed the entire crime. I dug madly through my pockets in case I missed any coins. I scanned the floor, hoping to find a penny that I could pick up, drop in the bowl, and then mumble something like, "Oh look at that . . . my penny must have bounced out onto the floor."

But no coins were to be found, and the reality set in that I was caught with my hand in the candy till. My panicked mind played various scenarios in high speed, each one worse than the next:

Would the customer tell Mr. Vitim?

Would Mr. Vitim tell my mother?

Would my mother tell my father? (that would mean far harsher consequences for me)

Would I be banned from Vitim's forever?

Was I at the top of a slippery slope leading to a career of crime, maybe escalating to bank robbery, or worse?

My train of thought leading to a stint in the slammer was interrupted when the eyewitness to the crime stepped up to the register, paid for his newspaper, flipped a penny in the bowl, and walked out—without so much as uttering a word to me or even looking at me. I wanted to apologize, but nothing came out of my mouth. I just put my head down and briskly left the store, choking on the hard candy I was sucking.

On the way home, I swore that I was a changed person. I thanked God for making things turn out this way. In exchange for His benevolence, I made a list of promises I would keep, which included repaying Mr. Vitim, keeping my room clean, taking the garbage out to the street on Tuesday morning, never making fun of my teacher behind her back, and really listening to whatever the priest said during Sunday sermons. The list was daunting. But as a reformed young man, I was going to do it all. And if I fell short, I was prepared to be struck dead by a bolt of lightning.

Well, I didn't fulfill on any of these promises for more than a week, and I soon stopped avoiding open spaces when the clouds darkened. But there is one promise I did live up to:

when I got up the gumption to step foot in Vitim's again, I came up with a new formula to make full restitution, with interest. *One candy out, THREE pennies in.* Life is good—I would be redeemed.

From that point on, I promised myself that I'd never take what isn't mine, even if no one was looking. Though I'd not yet heard the statement, "honesty is the best policy," life had proven it to me. The experience also taught me something that I could not have verbalized back then: sometimes it's better to allow people to make the mistake they made and just let it go, hoping that your kindness will teach a greater lesson than a scolding would.

This played out a few decades after the high-profile candy heist, when I found myself in another grocery store. This one was five hundred times the size of Vitim's. It was a typical crowded Saturday morning at Shaw's, a large New England grocery chain. After checking off the last item on my shopping list for the coming week, I pushed my cart toward checkout lane number four, which looked promising—there were only two people ahead of me. I wheeled into line and saw an elderly woman in the lead position. She slowly and methodically put each item from her cart onto the conveyor belt, apparently doing the math to tally the cost for the goods she'd gathered.

I perused a magazine on a nearby rack, looking up now and then to monitor the progress of the line. The woman had placed the last of her items on the belt, reached into her purse, and handed the cashier a carefully assembled stack of bills organized by denomination. She clearly had the shopping trip well planned and was going to make every penny count. But the best laid plans can go astray: a ten-dollar bill had slipped unnoticed from her hand and floated to the ground.

Upon learning from the cashier that she was ten dollars short, a mortified look swept across her face. She looked down and around for the errant bill. But there was no money in sight. That's because the gentleman in back of her had placed his foot over the bill, no doubt intending to pocket the dough on his way out. The woman frantically scanned the ground for another thirty seconds, then reached into her purse and pulled out ten singles to pay for her food.

I was shocked and saddened at what I had just witnessed. I felt sorry for the victim and sorry for the perpetrator, too. At an earlier time, I might have gotten angry, exposed the selfish and callous act, and embarrassed the guy with the sticky shoes into doing the right thing. But as I stood contemplating my options, a vision of the great candy caper at Vitim's came to me. I knew what I had to do.

Just as the elderly woman was gathering her bags, I reached into my wallet, took out a ten-spot, and squeezed past the man with the money under his foot. Without looking at him, I tapped the woman on her arm. "Excuse me, ma'am, I think you dropped this."

Ecstatic and visibly relieved, she thanked me profusely before heading toward the exit doors with her cart.

My actions in the checkout aisle, it turns out, were only part one of a beautiful unfolding moment. As I loaded my groceries into the trunk of my car, I felt a tap on my back. I turned around, and there was the fellow who'd appropriated the woman's money. He lowered his head and handed me the now-soiled ten-dollar bill. I heard a faint, "I'm sorry" just before he turned and quickly walked away.

The Great Vitim's Candy Caper readied me to appreciate the fact that either good action can conquer bad action, or it can't. Well, it just so happens, it can. The added bonus to doing what's best for all concerned, without any fanfare, is that nothing feels better to the human heart.

The myth I believed:

There's no harm to acting with a personal angle in mind.

The reality I discovered:

Honesty and integrity have no personal angles.

CHAPTER 4

Toeing the Line

—◈—

The myth I believed:

**Learn to fit in; play it safe—
it's right and proper.**

S mall towns, like the one where I grew up, survive because the pull of tradition is stronger than the outside forces that propel the younger generation into the larger world in search of excitement and prosperity. In our town, few people reached "escape velocity" and broke free of the gravitational forces holding them in place.

For me, as was the case of my parents and grandparents, simple rites of passage and admission to the "tribe" kept me from thinking beyond the town limits, let alone reaching for the stars.

One of the more unusual male traditions in our town was gaining recognition for adopting your father's gait. Townsfolk knew who a young man's dad was by his walk. It was a fingerprint. We young boys had plenty of practice at getting our father's unique gaits right. Each day after breakfast, at about 7:30 a.m., the dads walked their children to school. The men ambled on together at the head of the pack, and the boys walked behind them, much like waddling ducklings, struggling to keep up. The girls, including my sister Buffy, were part of the flock; but they were more interested in girl stuff, and had no interest in walking like their dads. We were dropped off at the corner of the street where the school was located, and the men continued on for a few blocks to report for work at the factory.

Each man had his own style of walking, some often accentuated by the clumsy steel-toed footgear they wore for work. My dad sort of lumbered along and flared his feet outward in the classic "duck-toe" style. Stevie Brown's dad had a slight limp that he got in the war. And Kenny's father had a heal-toe walk, almost robot-like.

At some point, probably around age ten, we boys had unconsciously mastered our dads' walking style and stride. Our bodies just knew what to do; and from there on, it was all muscle memory. I learned the outward flare, Stevie adopted a touch of a limp, and Kenny mastered the heel-toe walk. **Walk like Dad, be like Dad**; that was the unconscious command.

I remember the day that my father's friends noticed how much I walked like him. "Hey, Bob, look at Bobby; he's got you down perfect."

They laughed, and one of Dad's friends said, "Nice job, Bob. You've got yourself a young man there." Although I wasn't aware that I was literally following after Dad's footsteps, boy, was I proud to hear that!

My father beamed and told me I was in for a treat later that day when he got home from work. I did a double take, because this wonderful invitation came out of nowhere. What could it be?

What I didn't know was that another ritual was at play. When a father was complimented by being told that his son walked like him, he would treat his son to a special experience to honor the boy's first step into mature adulthood.

My dad decided to take me to Vitim's because he knew how much I loved their soda pop, especially when we sat at the counter together—father and son. When Dad got home from work, he washed up and said, "Let's go for a short walk." We set out on a journey together, feet splayed outward. This was exciting.

We arrived at Vitim's within ten minutes, and Dad said, "I'm going to have a coffee. Let's go to the counter, and you can get soda. Sounded great to me. I treasured these moments at Vitim's. Even though Dad always ordered the same thing—coffee for himself (Vitim's was known for good coffee), and a small ginger ale for me. On occasions when I had the pleasure of sitting in Vitim's with Dad, Mr. Vitim would stride up to us, look at my father, and say in a funny manner, "And what shall it be, sir?" My father would place the order, then hand Mr. Vitim a dime and a nickel.

On this special day, Mr. Vitim asked his usual question, and my dad pointed to me and said, "Ask Bobby."

Mr. Vitim nodded and smiled. He shifted a step over in my direction, looked me in the eyes, and asked, "And what shall it be, sir?"

"My dad will have a coffee, and I'll have my usual small ginger ale," I said proudly. Already, I felt empowered. I'd never gotten to order before! While Mr. Vitim made our drinks, my dad slipped me a dime and a nickel to give to Mr. Vitim when he came back. This was dizzying. I couldn't believe it. I was paying! A minute later, the two of us sat sipping our beverages, just two guys passing the time away.

When we got home, I told my mother about the remarkable field trip I just took with Dad. She beamed and patted my shoulder. At that moment, I was so proud to be a member of the family. The next day when I walked to school, I stayed behind my dad. But I was no longer just a kid on his way to elementary school. I was a young *man* on his way to elementary school. I felt good. For, along with the walk, there came a comfortable feeling that my destiny in our town was shaped and formed, and I need not worry about my future. At some unconscious level, I was probably thinking ahead to when I'd pass on the Bob White shuffle to my own children.

In junior high and high school, I continued walking like my dad, and began having similar conversations as my dad's. I enjoyed the thought of becoming an integral member of the community. I learned from my father that becoming a man also meant being fiscally responsible. He believed in paying your own way through life. My father told me, "A little hard work won't kill you," and I took his tip seriously. I wasn't afraid of working hard; in fact, I was proud to take on a paper route after school, mow lawns in the summer, and shovel snow in the winter.

In my junior year of high school, I was thrilled to land a plum job. New England Telephone Company had set up a depot in our town where fifteen trucks were maintained. That meant good pay from a respectable company. My job entailed cleaning up the trucks each day and making sure they had enough oil in the engine and air in the tires. Since there was a lot to keep track of, I made a chart that recorded when each truck was checked and the status of its oil and tire pressure. That seemed like the logical thing to do.

One day, Roy, the manager, took an interest in what I was doing. I liked Roy. He wore a tie, white shirt, and suede jacket—not the usual attire for townsfolk. Other than Sunday services and funerals, most men wore denim and work clothes. Our teachers wore ties and white shirts, but they had to. Roy not only dressed for success, he exuded confidence and ease in his manner. I liked his style.

Roy noticed the notebook I was carrying and asked me if he could see the chart I'd created. I showed it to him and said that having a checklist was my way of being sure I didn't miss a truck.

He flipped through the three pages of my chart and, without looking up, said, "Yup, you're college material, that's for sure. You know how to think on your feet. You'll go far." He raised his head, looked me in the eyes, smiled, and handed back the chart.

Wow! Talk about a disruptive moment. He didn't give me a motivational speech about going to college; he just *assumed* I was going. He assumed that *I* assumed I was going to college. Blow me over with a feather! I'd never assumed that. I never gave it any thought. I was a mill town boy. I expected to get a job in the local factory and maybe surpass my dad by rising above lineman and becoming a supervisor.

Me, college material? I must have looked like a deer staring down the proverbial headlights when Roy so casually mentioned me and college in the same breath. In the following weeks, the idea of going to college enticed me more and more. What if . . . ?

As I got more daring with my thoughts, I took an action step that was out of the ordinary for me. I was on my way to Doyle's Cuts for my next haircut. Doyle was the local barber on Main Street. His signature haircut looked like he put a bowl on your head and trimmed around the rim. He was also the only barber in town, so he enjoyed a captive market.

As I was walking to Doyle's for a quick snip, Tony (an older friend of mine) cruised by in his car. Tony pulled over and asked me if I wanted a ride. Of course I did. Who didn't want a ride with Tony? He was cool. I told Tony where I was going, and he said, "You gotta go over to Joe's barbershop. That guy doesn't just cut your hair, he styles it." Joe's shop was located in the next town over, and Tony offered to give me a ride.

"Let's do it," I said.

I was taken aback at first by the fact that Joe's head was as bald as a cue ball. *How could someone with no hair possibly be good at cutting hair?* I wondered. I remember thinking, *Geez, I'd wear a bag over my head if I was ever that bald.*

My concerns about Joe's credibility vanished when he twirled me around in the barber chair, studied my hair, and said, "I know *exactly* the style that will work for you. I call it 'the winner's cut.'"

I nodded, even though I had no idea what my hairless haircutter had in mind.

Joe clipped and snipped and jabbered while I sat wondering what in the world I'd look like. Twenty minutes later, he twirled me around again, this time so I could get a good look at myself in his full-length mirror. He waited a moment, allowing me to marvel at his creation.

He pointed at me in the mirror and said, "Now *that's* what a winner looks like."

I took the moment very seriously. This was awesome. Joe had created a new image for me. And I was ready to create a brand new version of myself that befitted the wavy locks now flowing smoothly over my ears. Although this transformation cost a dime more than the Doyle's bowl cut, I knew in my heart that it was well worth it.

When I got home that afternoon, I stood before the mirror in the bathroom and liked what I saw—a new look, and a whole a new me that was beginning to break free.

When my father arrived home from work and got a glimpse of my new haircut—was he ever angry! Not only had I broken with tradition—I'd spent an extra dime for such foolishness! Perhaps he was seeing that I was not going to follow the path he intended for me.

Well, it wasn't long after this winner's cut experience that I began wondering if I really wanted to work in the factory, or if I even wanted to live in our town all of my life. I was becoming curious about what might be possible beyond the town limits.

My curiosity was unusual for most kids I knew; we all pretty much subscribed to "flat-earth thinking"—don't go beyond the edge, or you'll fall into a great abyss. But in our version of "flat-earth thinking," the risk of exploration was more than falling into a great abyss; it also meant falling from grace and failing to abide by the unspoken laws that bound us together from generation to generation.

As I wrestled with the dueling forces of loyalty to my family and loyalty to myself—a centrifugal push and centripetal pull—a strange thing happened: I lost my acquired gait. I began to walk tall and straight. As I began thinking more about what might really lay beyond the edge of the world where I was born, I was discovering my own unique style of being.

The mere act of flirting with the idea of college, and getting my hair styled in a neighboring town, had me stepping beyond the boundaries of my comfort zone. This felt enticing and exciting. From here on, mine would be a life invented and reinvented, rather than a life cast in stone by those who came before me.

The myth I believed:

Learn to fit in; play it safe— it's right and proper.

The reality I discovered:

Be true to thyself—it's always right and beautiful.

CHAPTER 5

Standing Firm on Thin Ice

—◇—

The myth I believed:

I can wish, but I'm powerless to insist.

AND THEN I MET MARGARET

I n our town, probably like most towns, there was a hierarchy
of authority that children had to respect. The hierarchy was
like gravity, self-evident and unrelenting. Parents and police
officers were at the top of the pyramid. Teachers, priests, min-
isters, and others factored in, of course, but parents and the
law ruled.

This isn't to say that all kids did everything they were
told. To the contrary, like children everywhere, we continu-
ously tested the limits, pushing and probing to figure out where
the hard lines were really drawn in the sand. For me and my
best friend, Stevie, that meant going to forbidden places, like
the frozen banks of Miller's River in midwinter. Miller's River
was a rapidly flowing waterway that ran through town. During warmer days of winter thaws, huge ice formations pushed
out of the water, transforming the banks into a magical, other-
worldly scene—the most incredible playground that any curious twelve-year-old could possibly want. Our parents warned
us to stay away from the river. They told us a story of someone
fifty years ago who slipped on the ice, fell into the river, and
was swept away. They reminded us that we'd surely fall while
playing some harebrained game, like king of the iceberg, and
break a few bones—so "Stay away!"

Our fathers had good reason to believe that we'd toss cau-
tion to the wind and head for the icebergs, in spite of their
warnings, because that's what they did growing up. Why
would we be any different? King of the iceberg, iceberg tag,
iceberg high jump—the crazier and more dangerous the game,
the more we craved it! The fact that it was forbidden only made
it more alluring.

During one of our riverbank expeditions, Stevie and I
were in the midst of inventing a new game that involved leap-
ing from iceberg to iceberg while carrying a chunk of ice. We
both stopped when we spotted a female deer fifty or so feet

away. She was clearly in trouble. Her left front leg was stuck in between two pieces of ice, and she had a small laceration by her ankle. Deer have delicate ankles, and her sixth sense told her she had to gently extricate her hoof. But, as we approached, she started to panic and reared her hind legs, which only put her in a more precarious position.

"Don't get too close," I said to Stevie. "She might break her leg, and then someone will have to shoot her. It's like a horse that breaks its leg; it never recovers. We need help to free her. You go find some help, and I'll stay here."

Stevie said he was going to go ask his mother what to do. I wasn't so sure about that, since we weren't supposed to be down by the river, let alone iceberg hopping. I stood there thinking of alternatives; but after another moment of watching the deer struggle, I said, "All right, tell Lila. (Stevie's mother was special—she was the only adult I got to call by her first name.) I'll wait here. I hope she doesn't tell my mother." These were desperate times, so we had to take desperate measures.

After Stevie left, I sat with the deer, talking to her in a soft voice. "It's okay; we're going to get you some help. It's okay. As long as I'm here, no one's going to hurt you." I said, "As long as I'm here, no one's going to hurt you," three or four times.

Eventually, the deer calmed down. She seemed to almost understand what I said, and trust me, or at least realize that I wasn't dangerous. I could tell she was breathing normally. I really liked what we were doing—helping this poor deer.

Well, Lila called the police, and within ten minutes an officer arrived at her house, which was at the edge of the path that led to the riverbank. Stevie led the officer down to where I was waiting and pointed to the deer. The officer assessed the situation, and then said, "Boys, get on home," as he drew his gun from his holster. I'd never felt such a panic.

"What are you going to do?" I called out in alarm.

"I'm going to do what has to be done: shoot her," he said calmly.

"Are you crazy? You're not shooting her!" I screamed.

I got up and moved to within fifteen feet of the deer, positioning myself between the officer and his target. Oddly, the deer didn't panic with all the commotion.

"I can't let you shoot her. I promised her that, as long as I was here, she would be all right," I said in a calm voice.

Stevie looked on in disbelief, as if he was sitting in the front row seat at an action movie.

I expected harsh words, a lecture about obeying the law, and most certainly the threat of telling my parents. Maybe I'd be handcuffed and thrown in the back of the cop car. But, I still refused to move. I stood my ground.

To my amazement, the officer looked at me for a moment and then nodded his head respectfully. "Well, okay then," he said. "You're Bob White's son, aren't you? That's a pretty tall order you're taking on—keeping your promise to that deer. But she's only going to die out here if she doesn't get loose soon. And she'll suffer in pain while dying. I'll be back in an hour. If she's still stuck, I'm going to have to do it my way." With that, he holstered his weapon and headed up the embankment.

In that moment, though I was still a boy, I felt different on the inside. I felt like a man. I'd stood for something more than just wanting to play and have fun. I felt a different sensation inside of me, and I liked it. I'd stood firm for my word and didn't back down in spite of what could be terrible consequences. That was a major moment of truth for me. I felt like I'd taken a giant step from the earth to the moon and back again.

I turned around to approach the deer slowly, not sure what to do next. As I walked slowly toward her, talking with a calm, quiet voice, she once again began tugging her leg, but more slowly than before. When I was five feet or so from her,

I stopped talking, and just watched. I knew she didn't want me to get any closer. Within minutes, she was free!

Stevie and I gasped with relief when she stood on all fours, and we could see her foot was not injured. Gingerly, she padded over the ice, making her way onto solid ground. The two of us were quiet, just watching. The deer went up the hill about twenty yards and turned back toward us.

"Bobby!" Stevie exclaimed. "She's looking at you! She's saying thank you!"

As the deer disappeared into the woods, I felt a warm glow, which then turned to panic. Now I'd have to face the music at home. First of all, we were down at the river where we weren't supposed to be, and Lila and a policeman both knew it. Second, I disobeyed, even challenged, a police officer. This alone was grounds for a major punishment, like having to go directly home from school for a week, even a month. It would be the equivalent of house arrest.

But my good deed tipped the scales to the good side. Lila didn't say a word about it to my mother. The police officer didn't say anything, either. In a small town, news about misdeeds and miscreants travels quickly; I'd have heard if he'd made anything of it. The universe shined favorably upon me, as well as upon the deer, that day.

To this day, I wonder—did I help the deer, or did the deer help me have my first real experience of being my word, experiencing self-integrity? And, of course, then there's the police officer. He could see that my reactions were not for sake of appearances, but for the sake of what I thought was right. And he respected that.

Two years after the deer incident, I turned fourteen, which, in our town, meant coming of age. There was no special gala gathering; rather, fathers led their sons through the rite of passage by presenting them with their first hunting vest. At fourteen, boys weren't allowed to shoot or even carry a rifle, but they could accompany their fathers on deer hunting expeditions during deer season.

Every deer season, Dad was a pro at coming home with a good-sized doe strapped to the roof of the car. A trickle of fresh blood still glistened on the windshield by the time he got home, giving witness to the primal act that defined him as the provider of our family.

So my time had come to join the ranks of the deer hunters. As the big deer-hunting week approached, a week that my dad and many factory workers took off from work every year, he stopped at the local sporting goods store to pick up a hunting vest for me. I was sitting in the kitchen with my mother when he burst through the door, so excited he practically ripped the vest from the box.

"Try it on," he said. "Might be a little big, but you'll grow into it. We'll put it to good use, starting this weekend."

In that instant, I realized that I didn't want to try it on, because I didn't want to go deer hunting. My encounter with the deer a couple years back had changed my attitude completely about deer hunting. It really hadn't dawned on me until now. And another moment had come when I had to again stand for what I believed in. "I don't want to." This time I spoke shyly, not sure what would happen next.

"You *what*?" my father asked.

"I don't want to try it on. I don't want to go deer hunting," I said, as my mind flashed back to the beautiful creature I saved from the police officer's bullet.

My father was angry. He simply stormed out of the room and didn't talk to me for three days. Even my mother was taken by surprise. She'd never seen me stand so firm about something so entrenched in town tradition—dad and son going deer hunting.

I understood, back then, that my refusal was not an act of adolescent rebellion. What I didn't fully understand was that it was an inkling of a major shift in my way of thinking. I was beginning to question everything that was supposed to be the bedrock of my life then, and into the future. One thing was apparent to me: nothing would be the same from then on.

Later in college, while studying e. e. cummings, I came across one of his famous quotes, "Do I dare to be myself? To be nobody but myself in a world that does everything it can to make me like everyone else is the hardest battle any human can fight."

Looking back at my refusal to don the hunting vest, I see now—the battle had begun for me.

The myth I believed:

I can wish, but I'm powerless to insist.

The reality I discovered:

Stand for what I believe, and I have the power to persist.

CHAPTER 6

Fitting In

—◇—

The myth I believed:

**If you must choose between indecision
and perhaps making a wrong decision—
it's right to choose indecision.**

High school commencement was a big event in our small town. For most of the kids, it was the pinnacle of their formal education, and everyone knew that a high school diploma was needed to land a decent job at one of the two local factories.

Graduation was traditionally held on a Saturday, followed by congratulations and photo ops. The family barbecue and celebration that came next were part of the tradition, but the excitement began when the graduates got together at the lake at midnight and partied until the wee hours of the morning.

My class was ushered into the adult world under light clouds, a pale-blue sky, and a mild breeze. A collective cheer filled the air as all fifty-eight of us tossed our graduation caps into the air. Most cheered that they were free of any further formal schooling, but the guys knew that the real education was about to begin, starting with the orientation session at the factories. This took place on the following Wednesday. Up to that point, none of the male graduates knew which of the two factories would employ him. But, by the end of the day on Wednesday, the factory employment lists would be known. You would have thought there'd be flaws in the system, and the names on the factory lists would leak out ahead of time; but like the Academy Awards, that just didn't happen.

The day after Wednesday's orientation, the new factory inductees went off to work just as regularly as they attended school, but now they were getting paid for an honest day's work and suffering the consequences for being late or truant. Graduates who chose military duty after high school were guaranteed jobs at one of the plants when they returned.

I didn't get an invite to the big Wednesday affair because I was one of a handful of students who was going to college. Attending college was an unusual step for a community where almost everyone worked in the local factories. The high school guidance counselor, Mrs. Ebbs practically choked on her donut when I had asked her for information about colleges during the fall semester of my junior year. There were two reasons for her surprise.

First, the students who went to college were usually kids of the few professionals and business owners who lived within our town limits. These kids weren't really part of the main-stream of community life. We called them "mayflies," born amongst us but destined to fly away.

Second, and more baffling for Mrs. Ebbs, was the fact that I was exhibiting the potential to be major contender in our town, given my vehicular status and my skills at the billiard table.

In our corner of the world, if you had a car when you were sixteen, you had street cred with the twenty-somethings. If you were good at billiards and got along with everyone, you had "pool cred" with the fifty-somethings. I had worked hard and saved money to buy a car by my senior year, which my parents allowed me to buy because I needed a car to get to my after-school and weekend jobs (unskilled maintenance work, lawn mowing, and pumping gas). There was no public transporta-tion in our neck of the woods.

I was proud of the fact that I didn't have to depend on others for a ride. The car was a beater, but I loved it. Every day throughout my senior year, I drove the Mercury Montclair to school and to and from my various jobs. People noticed the am-bitious kid with the car; I was on the radar screen for achieving local success.

When I had time after work, I hung out at the local pool hall (equipped with ten pool tables and a few chairs). It was a clean-cut place, no alcohol. Pool was a big sport in our town; almost all the guys played pool. I loved honing my skills with a cue stick—not for sport, but as part of my short- and long-term economic plan. If I got good enough, I could make some money. And I did—sometimes five dollars in one night, which was a lot of money back then. More important, I didn't just play with my peers and the factory line workers. I saw to it that I was there on Thursday evenings, so I could pick my opponents strategically, challenging the plant supervisors. That was the night they showed up and took over the tables.

At first they were amused and thought I was just posturing—until their quarters started slipping from their pockets into my pocket. Playing against the power elite in the factories gave me a leg up, and it was my first experience learning how to play the system. Both factories in town vied to have me as an employee, especially given the important annual pool tournament between the companies.

Though I had applied to college, I was keeping my options open. I was highly motivated to become a candidate of choice for a good factory job. The positions came with different descriptions at different pay grades. The best jobs were on the fast track to the ranks of management. While many of my peers would depend on their dads (if they had influence) to get a better job, I was poising myself to get a plum position on the line and perhaps set a land-speed record from factory floor to management suite.

Although that would mean I'd bypass my dad—and he was a respected, hardworking soul—he couldn't have been more proud of me. He loved the strategy. "Two years to supervisor!" he boasted to his friends while patting me on the back. "*No one* has ever made it so fast!"

Given that backdrop, you'd have to ask why any sane person slated for knighthood, maybe even coronation, would contemplate leaving the kingdom?

Any that's exactly the question that Mrs. Ebbs wanted to ask back in my junior year, but she didn't. What she did do was blab it around that I was looking into going to college. Soon my friends had known about my college inquiry, but they laughed, thinking I was just pulling the guidance counselor's leg. In truth, I wasn't sure what I was doing initially, so I laughed along and pretended that's all I was doing—pulling her leg. The fact was—I was merely flirting with the idea of going to college in the beginning. The flirtation only escalated to a serious courtship, and then consummated the relationship when I learned in April of my senior year that I was accepted at the University of Massachusetts.

Everyone—including me—realized then that I was truly going to abandon everything I had going for me in town. And my decision had consequences.

"So, Bobby, you're off to be a hot-shot college boy. Will you still talk to us when you graduate from college?" That was the kind of ribbing I received from my friends. I took it in stride and in good humor, but I was nervous.

My father, in some way, felt betrayed. Before I was accepted into college, Dad used to share stories about his workday every evening as we ate supper, describing details as though he was preparing a future colleague. Now he didn't bother mentioning his work. It was as if I had opted out of a perfectly arranged marriage.

My relationship with my friends began to change further, especially when factory orientation arrived. If graduation was the beginning of a rift, the factory orientation became a fault line that eventually landed us in two different worlds. Suddenly all of my friends were young men, off to work at the assembly lines. They spoke enthusiastically about their new jobs and training programs. My buddies had permanent careers while I was scrambling to find any employment to tide me over until college started in the fall. At this point, their lives still seemed exciting; mine was boring.

To make matters worse, when I hung out with my old cronies, I was the odd man out. The conversation was always factory/work related, mostly about what transpired on the production lines. I felt like I was hanging out with my father and his work buddies. And, of course, their inside jokes made no sense to me. I had nothing to contribute to the conversation, and that only made me feel more isolated.

During those three months, I worked a couple of jobs to save money, on a road-asphalting crew by day and pumping gas by night. From an early age, I'd been taught to hold myself accountable for money, something that has served me well throughout my life. Not only was paying my own way part of my DNA, I was committed to paying for my education *without* any loans. If this college thing didn't work out, I didn't want to be saddled with debt. That would make matters even worse.

As I counted down the days to my first semester at the University of Massachusetts, a feeling of insecurity and confusion began growing. My reservations were less about my choice of schools or possible majors, and more about whether I made the right decision at all. I'd spent so much time finessing my way around town, I figured I'd be a shoo-in at the factories. And now I was tossing away that advantage. At the university, I'd be starting all over again. I wasn't even allowed to have a car as a freshman, and being pretty good at pool certainly wasn't going to get me any academic credits. I was losing my two medals of honor. Was it worth chucking everything? After all, I had no idea what I wanted to be when I grew up!

Later in life, I'd look back and realize that the tenacity and drive I cultivated in the mill town served me well in college, in my teaching career, and later as an entrepreneur and businessman. But as a seventeen-year-old about to leave for college, I felt helpless and deserted, even though I knew deep inside that this wasn't so.

When the day of my departure for college finally arrived, my parents drove me to the campus, dropped me off at the dorm, and made a quick exit (unlike most of the other parents, who lingered for a few hours before saying good-bye to their kids). My parents felt like they were on another planet and wanted to hightail it out of there as quickly as possible. My father had commented on how nice the cars were that the other parents were driving. My mother noted how differently they dressed from the people in our town. At the time, I was troubled by their hasty departure. Later, I learned from my mother that they left abruptly for my sake—they didn't want to embarrass me.

As I watched my parents disappear down the road leading from my dorm, I felt somewhat abandoned. I knew I was going to have to learn to look away from the old and familiar in order to start my life anew. And I knew it wasn't going to be easy. For one thing, I was raised with two sisters and two brothers, and I had lots of friends. Now I'd have to get a job and even work on weekends to pay my way through college. Clearly, I wasn't going to enjoy the luxury of retreating to the comfort of home and the joy of my friends except when the campus closed on holidays.

Despite my conviction to making it as a college student, I never doubted myself as much as I did during those early days on campus. To make matters worse, my dorm roommate never showed up. The dorm mother told me that he decided against college at the last minute. This made me feel even more alienated. I lay in bed, staring at the dorm room ceiling at night, wondering, *What have I done?*

I wasn't used to such quiet in the evenings when I lived at home. The other students were friendly enough, but I felt they'd peg me for someone didn't belong, once they learned where I grew up. At any moment I could be exposed for the kid from the other side of the tracks, the kid who was meant to be working with a lathe, not his brain.

I remember when I invented a credible past so I could impress the coeds. One of my classmates was from Newton, which I learned was a wealthy community. His father was a doctor. My classmate dressed well, presented well, and talked about the neighboring towns of Wellesley and Brookline. I took a cue. When I began flirting with classmates and one girl asked, "Where are you from?"

I answered, "Wellesley . . . and my family's in manufacturing." (This was true, just not in the way I implied.)

While my Wellesley charade seemed to work, it just made me feel more estranged. I was living a lie, and that had to change. What I did next came most naturally to me. Instead of hanging out with the other students, I made friends with the dorm custodian, Pete. I found it easy to be around Pete because I didn't feel awkward about my hometown. He came from a small town pretty much like the one I just left. He was interesting, and he loved to play pool. We never actually played pool together, but our common interest made me feel comfortable.

During my many conversations with Pete, I learned that he was a great outfielder in high school and almost played pro baseball. Sadly, he explained to me, "My dumb antics got me bounced from the minor leagues, and I retreated to what my father has done all of his life—push a mop.

In order to spend more time with my newfound basement buddy, I created a schedule that allowed me to take courses, do some studying, flip burgers at the student commons, and visit with Pete a few times a week while he was working. Back then, there were no formal work-study program at the college, but I'd learned well from my high school days how to deftly juggle part-time jobs and school.

Stepping out of the mainstream of campus life and descending to the basement to chat with Pete was relaxing for me. I'd sort of recreated the life I lived while in high school. My new comfort zone was short-lived, though. After a few months, Pete did me a great favor; he said, "Bobby, you came to college so you wouldn't have to push a broom around for a lifetime. I enjoy your company, but you're missing the point of being here. You need to let go of your past and start mingling with your classmates. The school wouldn't have accepted you if you didn't belong here. Stop wasting time hanging out with me. It's time to get on with your life. I missed my chance—don't you miss yours."

He walked out of his office, mop in hand and gave me a big smile. I sat there for a few minutes gazing at Pete's tools and cleaning supplies. And then, I flipped off the light switch and shut the door. After walking back to my dorm room and turning the doorknob, I stopped abruptly as I stepped over the threshold. The significance of what had just happened struck me like a bolt of lightning: a door to one world had finally closed, and it was time for me to open another door. I still felt scared, but I knew it was time to muster up the courage to march toward a better life right then.

Over time, my interest in sitting with Pete faded as I made new friends, many of whom are still good buddies today. The lesson that this time in my life taught me is this: a new world exists for anyone who wants it, as surely as there are different continents on this planet.

Later, after graduating from college and securing a teaching position, I was working with a high school summer math class geared for students who were slated for college. They were all promising kids who needed a little help. One student, Malcolm, was an interesting study. He was very intelligent and good at math when he wanted to be, but he had a flippant attitude with his classmates and with me.

Malcolm passed his math tests easily, but when it came to handing in his homework assignments, he just laughed and made a wisecrack. Eventually I asked Malcolm if he'd mind having a chat with me after class. He reluctantly agreed. After some small talk, I told Malcolm that he was a very intelligent young man and I suspected he could go far in life if he wanted to. I asked him if he had any dreams for the future. I learned that he lived in a rough part of the city, and that all of his peers made fun of him for wanting to be an architect.

When I heard this, I immediately realized that Malcolm was caught between two worlds, just like I was when I entered college. I told Malcolm about my experience during the summer before going to college and the first few months of my freshman year. I told him about Pete, the custodian, and what I'd learned from him. I went on to say that the advanced math class setting was a perfect opportunity for him to begin making new friends—friends who would believe in him and support his dream enthusiastically. I told him that it might feel awkward at first, but in the end it would prove to be one of the wisest decisions he could make.

I further explained that not only does the company we keep define who we are, it also helps us determine the level of faith we have in ourselves. This is why I wanted to impress upon Malcolm that it was imperative that he choose his friends carefully and never stop daring to dream big. I remember ending my conversation by saying, "Malcolm the architect, I like how it sounds. I can see you being an architect, Malcolm. Can you?" He nodded his head and shuffled out of the room.

A few years later, I ran into Malcolm's mom at the local post office. (I'd met her when Malcolm enrolled in summer school). I asked her how Malcolm was doing, and she said exuberantly, "He's graduating from college in June and plans to get his master's degree in architecture. He wants to design beautiful office buildings."

I thought to myself, Malcolm's dream of designing beautiful office buildings will surely help him build a better life for himself.

I still feel grateful to Pete for helping me build a better life for myself. He was the first teacher that UMass offered me, and he wasn't even in the course catalogue! Pete didn't have a PhD and, in fact, never went to college. His was an underground course—literally, held in the basement of my dorm. If I met Pete today, I would bestow an honorary DOL (Doctor of Life) on him.

The myth I believed:

If you must choose between indecision and perhaps making a wrong decision— it's right to choose indecision.

The reality I discovered:

The very daring to decide and learn from one's decisions—that's always right.

CHAPTER 7

Shakespeare in My Left Pants Pocket

The myth I believed:

Cheating is sometimes the only way to beat the system and win.

I couldn't believe it was already 2:00 in the morning, and I was still on Chaucer! Just seven hours to go before my final exam in English Lit 101! With NoDoz, I might be able to finish writing my tiny crib sheets for each of the authors we studied in class, carefully listing their works and their major themes.

When I signed up for the literature course, I figured it would be easy sailing. I'd read of the great authors in high school English, so how hard could it be? Actually, how naïve could I be? I didn't bother to check out the reputations of various professors before registering for their courses. Some were considered soft touches, and some were called tough. Dr. Tucker, the English professor teaching this course was nicknamed "The Executioner." It was rumored that he was the reason many students flunked out of college. I'd not heard his nickname until I was well into the course, and it was too late to change courses.

C'mon, how bad could this guy be? I asked myself.

I found out when I took my midterm. I thought I'd done well. Dr. Tucker had a different opinion. I got C-minus. The test results sent shock waves up my spine, and I convinced myself that I'd surely flunk the final. I imagined my shame if I'd had to go to Pete and ask if he could get me a full-time custodial job at the college—there was no way I'd be able to show my face at home again.

I couldn't let that happen, so I decided to take the prudent course of action: I would cheat. I got this idea from Norman, a senior I'd met at the library. I'd go to the periodicals room a few times a week to study, and noticed Norman was always there—not studying, but using the tranquil, quiet environment to nap. Norman was known for his partying and lazy personality, but he was nonetheless well dressed and successful in his courses.

What's his secret? I wondered. So one day I introduced myself and asked him how he did it. He opened his eyes and expressed suspicion. Then looked around to see if anyone was watching, leaned into to me, and pulled a tiny piece of paper out of his wallet. It was a crib sheet. "If you can't beat 'em, cheat 'em," he whispered.

That's when I hatched the idea of transcribing my course notebook onto tiny pieces of paper, carefully organized by author and strategically placed in various pockets, starting with "C" for Chaucer. Shakespeare wound up in my rear pants pockets. I constantly tested myself—not about the course content, but about making sure I knew where to find the right crib sheet.

"Easy, Bobby," I reminded myself. "Shakespeare's got you covered—rear left."

Exam time rolled around, and I was wired with enough adrenaline energy and NoDoz to keep the entire campus lit up for three days. After collecting a blue book and taking my seat in the last row (I always sat in the back, so I wouldn't be noticed or called on), I had a moment of guilt. I knew that cheating was wrong, but I'd rationalized my plan by reframing the need to cheat as a necessary evil. Didn't I deserve *some* special dispensation for being the kid from the wrong place? Besides, they should've put a warning sign in the course catalog, you know, maybe with a picture of a guillotine? Fair's fair.

With pen poised, I dove into the exam and knew exactly where to find the right crib sheet. I glanced down casually and then up at the ceiling as if I were formulating a brilliant thought, then madly write down my answer. The first two questions went without a hitch.

Hey, this is a piece of cake, I thought. *What a dope I was for being so worried.*

Dr. Tucker was sitting at his desk in front of the room reading a journal, clueless about my illicit activities in the back row.

As I began the third question and carefully pulled out the card from my right front pants pocket, I noticed that Dr. Tucker wasn't even in the room.

Lucky break, I thought to myself. *He must really trust us.*

The thought about trust triggered an instant pang of guilt.

When that subsided, I realized I'd make a classic rookie mistake: failing to take into account the fact that there were *two* doors in the room. Dr. Tucker had merely exited the door at the *front* of the class and had circled around to the *rear* door, which had an unobstructed view of the last row.

I saw Dr. Tucker's shadow looming over my desk before I actually saw the man himself. I expected him to reach over and grab the evidence for all to see, then physically boot me out of the room to the jeering of my peers, "Cheater White couldn't write! Cheater White not so bright!"

Instead, he leaned down and whispered in my ear, "Mr. White, how can you possibly read such small print without a magnifying glass?"

Dr. Tucker slid my blue book off the desk, carried it to the front of the room, and put it in his briefcase. No one else noticed that I was busted; they were too busy finishing their exams the old-fashioned way.

What was I supposed to do? Walk out and hope that anyone who glanced up would think I was so fast that I'd turned in my exam early? Sit there hunched over my desk, like everyone else, and hope that no one noticed that the main difference between my desk and theirs was the lack of a blue book? I chose the latter, and the remaining thirty-five minutes seemed like a preview of hell. My mind tortured me with every scenario possible, and then some.

Oh my God! This is it. I'm done. I didn't even get through my first semester, and I've been tossed out of college for cheating. That's even worse than getting fired at one of the factories in my hometown for showing up drunk. I'll be drafted and sent into combat for sure. I'm ruined!

After what seemed like hours of mental torture, the bell finally rang. Everyone got up and formed a line that went by Dr. Tucker's desk. Each person dropped off his or her blue book. I got in the line and walked toward the desk like I was also going to turn in my test, too.

As I passed by the desk, Dr. Tucker said, "Mr. White, would you please stand aside for a moment? I want to speak with you."

Oh no, here comes the axe, I moaned inside.

A minute later, it was just the two of us. Dr. Tucker said absolutely nothing as he neatly gathered the test papers and put them in his briefcase. The silence was excruciating. He finally looked up and said, "I want to see you in my office tomorrow morning at eleven o'clock. And bring all your cheat sheets with you." With that, he walked out of the room and never glanced back.

What followed was the longest twenty-four hours in the history of the world. I avoided all of my new, soon-to-be ex-college friends for the rest of the day. I said I was feeling sick and needed to lie down. I did lie down; but, as much as my body craved sleep, my brain was in high gear, designing every excuse I could possibly give Dr. Tucker. I finally dozed off, but not before admitting to myself that I had no excuse, and that I probably just blew my one chance in life.

At the appointed time for my trial and execution, I walked into Dr. Tucker's office. He was busy correcting papers and barely glanced up at me. I noticed how impeccable he kept his desk and modest office. Each wall was adorned with a floor-to-ceiling bookcase with books and papers carefully arranged on the shelves.

A minute later, Dr. Tucker looked up and pointed to a chair by a small table under the window. I fetched the chair and sat down across from him, but I couldn't take my eyes off the floor.

"Look at me, Mr. White," he said firmly, but gently.

I raised my head as far as I could. "Give me your cheat sheets," he commanded.

I obliged, after which he spent a few minutes scanning through the notes. He then looked at me, and his demeanor changed. He asked me, in a softer voice, where I was from, what my dad did for a living, and what my reason was for wanting to attend college.

I answered the first two questions easily, but the last one threw me. I wasn't sure what I wanted to do. I wound up blurting out that I wanted to go to college because I wanted to learn to live my own life, and not necessarily do what my father and my grandfather did.

I wasn't expecting much sympathy, but I really wasn't prepared for Dr. Tucker's response. "You must be pretty smart to cram all of this information on such a small piece of paper. And it shows that you really took a lot of good notes—apparently, you understand the material. So, why on earth did you feel the needed to cheat? And how did you know which pocket to reach for to get the information you needed?"

I felt stupid and too ashamed to say anything. I also knew that whatever I said would just sound lame. So, I sucked in my gut and explained my alphabetical system of placing the authors in my shirt and pants pockets, and said I cheated because I'd barely passed the midterm exam and was afraid of flunking the final.

Dr. Tucker just stared at me. I thought I was surely finished, but he threw me a curve ball by handing me a new exam and blue book, saying, "Let's see how you would have done had you taken the exam legitimately. Go over to the table by the window and take the exam—you've got fifty minutes, Mr. White."

I almost filled the entire blue book while he continued to correct papers. When the time was up, I handed it to him and he asked me to sit down while he read it. Ten minutes later, he told me that I would have received a B-plus. Then came yet another surprise: he told me that he'd never done this before, but he was going to pass me with a C-minus on the exam. "Take a long walk around the campus, Bob, and ponder what just happened here today," he said. "This is not about me, it's about you. You can use your brain correctly, or you can use it to destroy your life."

I did just that. I took a very long walk. I cried. I laughed. I sang. I yelled angrily at myself. This man, who, it was said, never gave any student a break, had a huge heart. He'd given me a second chance.

And I would repay his kindness in two ways. First, I pledged to myself that I would set aside more time every day to study, no matter what exciting things were happening on campus. Second, I would prove to myself and to him that his consideration and tolerance for my misbehavior really would make a positive difference in my life.

The next semester I signed up to take English Lit 101 again with Dr. Tucker—not for credit—but as an extra course. I wanted to show him and prove to myself that I knew how to use my brain correctly, and that I intended to. I sat in the front row, fully participated in class discussions, passed all the tests, and received an A-minus in the course.

Even though the grade didn't hit my transcript, it represented a pivotal victory. Dr. Tucker sensed my pride and knew he was an important part of it. Maybe that's why he invited me to lunch at the end of the semester, something he never did with his students. To me, that was like passing the course with honors. As frosting on the cake, Dr. Tucker loosened up during the meal and even joked, saying, "Regarding those crib sheets of yours, Bob . . . you put Shakespeare in your left ass pocket?!"

Twelve years after graduating, I was teaching in Boston and living in an apartment with a roommate. I'd just sprung for a decent car, a three-year-old Plymouth Fury in pristine condition. I always parked it on the street in front of the building where I could keep an eye on it.

One summer evening, around 9:00 p.m., I decided to go out for a quick ride. As I walked out the front door, I was shocked to see someone bent over the front seat and rifling through my glove compartment. "Call the cops," I screamed, "Someone's trying to steal my car!"

The would-be thief got out of the car and, oddly enough, stood frozen, rather than beating a hasty escape. My roommate heard me yelling and called the police.

As I calmed down, I look directly into the face of this culprit, only to find that he was a young teenager. His eyes were locked onto his shoes. He was trembling.

Suddenly, I was sitting before Dr. Tucker, looking down at the floor and feeling so humiliated and ashamed for my own stupid action. I imagine that I looked just like the kid who was now standing in front of me.

"What am I going to do with you?" I heard myself say.

I asked similar questions that Dr. Tucker had asked me. They just came out of my mouth. "Where do you live?" and "What does your father do for a living?"

He told me that he lived in a housing project located about a mile away, and that he didn't have a father. Before I could say anything else, a cruiser had pulled up with its lights flashing. A police officer got out and asked what was going on. I said, "It was a misunderstanding. Everything's okay. Really sorry that I called you. I should have thought before I reacted."

The officer was annoyed, paused a minute, and then scolded me for causing an unnecessary police visit. He stared at the teenager, suspecting there was more to the story, but we all stood dead silent.

The officer returned to his car and drove off.

When the cruiser was out of sight, I said to the kid in a firm voice, "Now get out of here, and don't make that foolish mistake again! You look like a smart kid. Learn to use your brain correctly."

He was just as astonished by the outcome as I was after my encounter with The Executioner. He ran off, hopefully contemplating the lucky break life had just given him.

Six months later, I went into a local corner store to pick up some bread and eggs, and there was the same kid, stocking shelves. I nodded and said "Hi" to him.

At first he didn't know whether to run or remain mute. He did nod and awkwardly uttered something resembling "Hello."

I told the store manager that his helper seemed like a nice kid, and I asked how long he'd been working there. The manager said that he was a great kid, came from a tough neighborhood, and was never late for work. He'd been working part-time there for a few months.

As I left the store, I was reminded of how grateful I felt for the incredible gift Dr. Tucker gave me—gave the two of us, actually.

The myth I believed:

Cheating is sometimes the only way to beat the system and win.

The reality I discovered:

Win without compromising self-integrity—or there is no win.

CHAPTER 8

A Little Trick I Like to Call "Pay Attention"

—◆—

The myth I believed:

Just get it done—that's good enough.

As it turned out, my skill at pool actually did come in handy. Playing pool gave me "book money" each semester and put some extra change in my pocket. This talent was not enough, however, to cover all my college expenses.

When my freshman year came to an end, I decided to remain on campus over the summer and make as much money as I could toward my sophomore year's tuition, books, and board. I heard through the grapevine there were openings with the landscaping crew, but I'd have to sign up quickly if I wanted to snag one.

The college buildings sprawled across 500 acres, and the campus was known for its beautiful landscape. Even I appreciated the fifty-year-old rose bushes and rhododendrons.

So I made a beeline for the grounds maintenance office and asked if I could fill out an application. The secretary told me that Mr. Lampkin was in charge of all applications, and that his office was in the back, behind the tractors and mowers.

When I knocked on the office door, a voice yelled, "It's open." I walked in and found myself facing a tall, thin, rugged looking man, probably seventy or so. He was sitting at what looked like an army surplus desk. Although he was up there in years, he was fit and feisty, befitting of the US Marine Corp tattoo on his bicep. "What can I do you for?" he asked without looking up from his paper.

I told him I was looking for Mr. Lampkin so I could apply for a summer landscaping job.

"You're looking right at him," he said. "What qualifies you to work on my crew?"

I proceeded to tell him that nothing qualified me other than being a hard worker who wasn't afraid to get my hands dirty.

"Hands dirty! Of course you're going to get your hands dirty—it's landscaping," he responded with a laugh. "I assume you go to school here."

I told him I was finishing my freshman year, and then said, "I love the landscaping on campus, and would consider it an honor to help keep it trimmed properly."

Bingo—I'd pushed the right button.

"You'll start the day after your last final exam. I'll see you then. Report back right here at 8:00 a.m." Mr. Lampkin proceeded to hand me an index card from his desk drawer and said, "Write your full name on this card."

When I handed it back to him, he read it, and said, "Bob White—there's a quail down the cape that they call 'bobwhite.' Are you related?" Before I could come up with a clever answer, he said, "I'll see you next month, Bob." As he stuck the card in a filing index box. That was the shortest application I've ever filled out.

Over the next month, I learned that Mr. Lampkin was an institution unto himself. He was the top official presiding over the grounds; he'd worked at the university for more than four decades and was highly respected. Word had it that he was intimately acquainted with every leaf on every bush, and every thorn on every rose. If it was green, he could tell you its origins and history. Apparently, he took serious exception to anyone messing with the plant life in his care—especially the summer grounds crew. I also learned that his USMC tattoo was symbolic of the rules and the honor system that he so respected. He was a man who believed in following protocols and working hard, and he expected nothing less from anyone under him.

On the first day of my employment, Mr. Lampkin assembled his summer crew (nine students, in addition to his usual eleven full-time guys) in front of the maintenance headquarters building. He had the full-time workers introduce themselves and then sent them on their way to take care of tree trimming and other things they were hired to do.

Now, Mr. Lampkin wasn't at all harsh or mean, but he nonetheless proceeded to walk up and down like a drill sergeant assessing his new ragtag recruits. It felt like we were being inducted into the Army, with one major difference: we were going to be trained to defend our foliage against disarray and six-legged enemies; and our drill sergeant was decked out in denim overalls, a Boston Red Sox baseball cap, and muddy work boots.

After a few minutes, he announced, "My name is Patrick Lampkin. Just as you call your teachers 'doctor' or 'professor,' you'll call me *Mister* Lampkin." He then proceeded to tell us about the incredible variety of vintage shrubs and trees that had been around for many decades, and how much they were part of the university's heritage. We were to take great pride when pruning, "only cut by hand, and look for the *v*'s. Clean cuts. Never pull or yank anything. Mow the lawn in straight lines." And so on.

We might have gotten a little bored with his long dissertation, except for one thing: Mr. Lampkin had an odd figure of speech, one that struck our funny bones and curiosity zones. Any time he wanted to convey a key point, he prefaced it with "Let me put it this way." It was a smart tactic. Communication experts would call his verbal maneuver "flagging." A "flag" is a phrase that shakes us out of our immediate train of thought. It says, "Hey, dumbo, listen up and wake up—something big's coming at ya!"

It was especially important that we listened to what came next, after he said, "Let me put it this way," because he made it very clear that we were allowed one screwup. "Misshape a bush or miscut a lawn once, and it's a reprimand. Twice, and you're shown the door."

Curiously, the verbal flagging seemed to work. During the first week of work, if someone forgot what we were told to do that day, another crew member would say, "Let me put it this way," and repeat whatever Mr. Lampkin said earlier.

"Let me put it this way" became our hallmark phrase that summer. We'd even use it jokingly when we'd go for a bite to eat after work. "Let me put it this way," we'd say to the waitress, "I want a cheeseburger, and I'll accept nothing less."

One day, Mr. Lampkin made a rare tactical mistake. He told us to use the hedge clippers to trim the hedges that flanked the steps in front of the building that housed the dean's office. He probably figured we'd have enough horse sense to stop before the clippers hit the prized rose bushes at the end of the hedge. That bush had to be trimmed by hand.

Apparently, horses have more sense than we did; because Eddie, one of the crew, did a clean sweep of the left hedge from top to bottom, then continued beyond the hedge and began butchering the rose bush. Within seconds, half the rose bush looked like a mutant bonsai, just a wisp of its former incarnation.

I screamed, "Stop, Ed!" before Eddie massacred the entire bush. Eddie snapped to when he heard me scream, at which point he saw what he'd done. "Do you, uh, think Mr. Lampkin will notice?" he asked with a gulp.

"Notice?" I shrieked, "The man knows every bud on that bush and every bush on campus like the veins on the back of his hand. He'll be chasing you around campus with the hedge clippers when he sees it. We're all screwed!"

The words were barely out of my mouth when we saw a tall figure in blue overalls and muddy boots crouching down by the massacred rose bush, almost as if he was waiting for it to magically grow back. Mr. Lampkin sat down and put his head in his hands. Clearly he was upset.

"Those are the dean's favorite roses. When they're bloomin', they're the highlight of his day. Some of the board members have been looking to force me into retirement . . . they say I'm too old. This might be the excuse they need to get me out." With that, he got up, climbed the stairs of the building, and proceeded to the dean's office.

The three of us froze in place, silent.

Ten minutes later Mr. Lampkin walked down the steps. Without making eye contact with any of us, he said, "I want everyone to report to the maintenance building in ten minutes. Thank you."

He shuffled across campus, fanning himself with his Red Sox cap.

The three of us knew that the stupid mistake was all our fault, although no one pointed to Eddie, directly. We agreed that we should try to speak with the dean and explain that our careless behavior wasn't at all Mr. Lampkin's fault. We asked the dean's secretary if there was any chance we could see him for a minute.

"Does this have anything to do with the rose bush incident?" she asked.

Our answer gained us quick audience with the dean.

"It was me," Eddie blurted out as soon as we got in the dean's office. "I didn't pay attention to what I was doing even though Mr. Lampkin told me to be careful."

"Well, I'm pretty unhappy, and I appreciate your coming in to tell me exactly how it happened. If I live long enough, the rose bush will grow back to its full glory. Thank you for your honesty, men. Mr. Lampkin came in here and went to bat for all of you. He's quite a guy, isn't he?"

The dean then went back to what he was doing and without looking up asked, "Is there something else?" signaling that the matter was closed, and it was time for us to leave.

We assembled in front of the maintenance building as Mr. Lampkin instructed and found his demeanor to be just as it always was—firm, but gentle. No ranting or raving. No threats. No reprimands. He just talked about the proper way to trim a hedge and how to recognize a rose bush that hadn't yet blossomed. There **was** one subtle difference in his vernacular, though. "Let me put it this way . . ." had a new sidekick: "I have a little trick I like to call, 'PAY AT-TENTION.' I've never met anyone who succeeded in life and didn't pay attention."

Mr. Lampkin's final words stuck with me long after my adventure in the campus foliage, and no doubt contributed to my business success. Who would have thought that I'd have the opportunity to repeat them twenty years later in a very different setting in downtown Boston? I'd just opened my new restaurant, Devon on the Commons, and found myself facing an irate patron who demanded to see the owner. He was quite upset that his salad came with onions, even though he specifically told the waiter, "NO onions." He explained that he was allergic to onions, and they made him quite ill.

I apologized sincerely and ordered him a replacement salad, *sans* onions, and took the salad off his tab.

After closing that evening, I assembled the waitstaff. I wasn't wearing blue overalls or muddy boots, but I did borrow from Mr. Lampkin and said, "Let me put it this way . . . the customer's always right; and if you see to it that he feels that way, no matter what the situation may be—we have a loyal customer."

The offending waiter became a tad defensive and explained that it was a mistake. "So the guy accidentally got onions. He wasn't going to choke and die. Besides, he got a free salad out of it."

I stood still for a moment, thinking about how Mr. Lampkin would handle this matter. I looked at the waiter and calmly said, "I have a little trick I like to call 'pay attention.' Pay attention to your customer's needs, and your customer will pay attention to the size of the tip he gives you. In fact, I've yet to meet anyone who is successful in life who doesn't pay attention." That grabbed the waiter's and the rest of the staff's attention.

The Lampkin lexicon worked its way into the Devon lexicon. Everyone began paying better attention, so much so that the Lampkin way of doing good work became the Devon way of doing good business.

The myth I believed:

Just get it done—that's good enough.

The reality I discovered:

Pay attention and do your best—that's what's good enough.

CHAPTER 9

Craving a Lilac Mint

❖

The myth I believed:

Only the few are selected to win.

"Would you like one?" the woman asked, opening an elegant tin, filled with mints.

I hesitated.

"Go ahead, it's okay," she assured me.

So I popped the mint into my mouth, and my eyes must have lit up.

"Lilacs aren't just for sniffing; they taste good, too," she said, pointing to the lavender-colored bushes that graced the grounds surrounding us.

This interchange took place on a warm, sunny day in Hyannis Port during the summer between my junior and senior year of college. At the time, I was renting a cottage with some college friends, and a few of us hadn't yet found steady summer employment. But we had an "in." My roommate, Carl, knew one of the security guards at a magnificent estate on the ocean, a half-mile down the road from where we were staying. The guard helped us snag a one-day gig, serving appetizers at an outdoor spring bash, attended by 160 social elites.

Other than the fact that the uniform I was given was absurdly mismatched for my body—shirt too small, vest too big, pants too long—it seemed like a great way to make some quick money on a warm summer day. Besides, who wouldn't want to be a fly on the wall at a big Hyannis social event?

The caterer told us what to do, and we set about roaming the lawn with trays of appetizers, reloading when empty. That was the easy part; the hard part was feeling comfortable in the midst of people who I thought were way out of my league. From their pressed linen pants, skirts, crisp button-down shirts, and blouses, to their shimmering Harvard, Yale, and Princeton class rings, these were tomorrow's movers and shakers. I was certain I was offering salmon puffs to future business leaders and legislators. Maybe even a potential president or two. The only thing they'd remember about me was the ridiculous uniform I was wearing and perhaps the scent of salmon puffs I was acquiring from the hors d'oeuvres.

When it was time for my break, I walked off to the far corner of the lawn to relax and look out at the ocean. I felt envious and intimidated. I came from a place where a backyard barbecue and a cold Bud were as good as it gets. I felt like an outsider gazing into a world where I'd never be welcome.

As I stood, gazing at the water, an older woman casually walked over, folded her arms, and began watching the party guests. She was dressed in a pink, silk summer suit, and she carried herself with grace and sophistication. I thought perhaps she was a rich neighbor who might have wandered over to briefly enjoy the event. She seemed kindly and nonthreatening. Even so, I was startled when she offered me that mint and asked my name. She went on to ask what I did when I wasn't serving up appetizers.

I told her I was attending college, and that this was my first time as a server. She commended me for getting out there in the world and doing what it takes to earn a living. Everyone else was so aloof, but this woman treated me as if I were an invited guest.

I was grateful that she saw beyond the ill-fitting clothing. Still, she had good radar and sensed that I felt out of place. Many of the people I was serving were not much older than me, yet they were on the launch pad for stellar success.

"They look so impressive, don't they?" she asked.

"Oh yes," I replied. "They certainly do."

"How many of them do you think will actually achieve their goals?"

"Why, all of them."

"I'd say three will."

"What?" I said. "How's that possible? These people are the cream of the crop in every way."

"Oh, they're all ambitious, and they all have wonderful

dreams, and many come from successful families. But deep down, most of them are nervous that their contacts will fall through or their plans will fail. No matter how confident they're acting, they don't trust their personal judgment when it's time to make important decisions. So they'll settle for far less than what they really want out of life.

I was dumbstruck. Even people with stellar family pedigrees and Ivy League educations could fall short of their goals simply because they didn't trust their own judgment or because they worry about their plans failing? And the ability to succeed isn't because of lineage or upbringing.

This revelation sparked a change in my thinking. It caused me to completely recalibrate my understanding of the world's pecking order. All of a sudden, the playing field was a little more level. Perhaps I had a right to be in the game if I developed faith in myself, regardless of my less-than-aristocratic roots.

A successful life is built on self-confidence," the elderly woman went on to say. She then quietly walked away.

On the way back to the cottage, I told Carl about the woman I was chatting with, he laughed and said, "I noticed you two chatting. Do you know who she is?"

"Why would I know? I don't live around here," I replied.

"You were talking to Rose Kennedy! Know who *she* is?"

Damn, I thought, smacking my head. *How dumb of me!* There I was getting advice from a wise woman who was known for teaching her own children self-confidence and the importance of trusting their judgment when it came to pursuing their plans. She certainly inspired her children to waste no time doubting themselves, and she put a good dose of that wisdom in my mind that day, too.

Ten years after the summer catering gig at the Kennedy compound, I had a new gig of my own. I was now teaching and took a job supervising ten teenagers who were enrolled in the city's youth summer work program. Their job was to remove all the desks and furniture from classrooms in one of the schools, so the custodians could wash, wax, and buff the floors. The school had sixty classrooms, and the floor-waxing project was expected to take six weeks.

Four of the five boys knew each other and got along well. They talked and laughed together, and acted like they were kings of the hill, not unusual for teenage boys to do. Jose, on the other hand, kept to himself. He was courteous and a hard worker. He was not only more focused than the other four boys combined, he was also careful getting out the furniture without denting the wood or scratching the floor. I had to monitor the others to minimize damage to the furniture and the premises.

Not surprisingly, the other kids pretty much ignored Jose. During breaks, he stood aside and shyly observed their antics.

One day, when I noticed him eating lunch alone, it occurred to me that he probably felt very much like I did that summer day when I met Rose Kennedy in Hyannis Port. I didn't have a lilac mint to offer, but I sat down beside him and offered some potato chips from my lunch. He appreciated the gesture. I asked him how many of these kids he thought would be successful when they got out of high school.

He quickly said, "All of them. They're really cool."

I paraphrased what Mrs. Kennedy said to me: although they seemed pretty sure of themselves and considered themselves to be at the top of the heap, they probably wouldn't end up pursuing their real dreams. Why? Because even though they act really cool on the outside, they felt insecure and unsure of themselves on the inside.

I looked Jose in the eye and said, "You're a diligent worker, Jose, and you take pride in doing your job well. I feel confident that you're going to make right decisions, and be successful when you finish school. If you start feeling as confident about your future as I do, I believe you've got a great life ahead of you. Don't sell yourself short, Jose."

There was a moment of silence. I'd passed along Rose Kennedy's inspiring message in my own style, and I felt that he took it seriously.

Fast forward another fifteen years. I'd left teaching and was doing very well in the real estate development business. I needed an electrician to rewire an old building that I purchased for renovation. My usual electrician, Jim, was moving to Florida; and before leaving, he recommended an electrician friend that had worked for him part-time for a few years before starting his own company. When the truck pulled up, I couldn't believe who jumped out of the driver's seat: Jose!

Jose was now a licensed electrician, had branched out on his own, and had his own business with two trucks and four employees. Beneath his name on the truck were the words. "Master Electrician—I'll never leave you in the dark."

I congratulated him with a big smile, at which point he said, "Do you remember that day when I was working for you, moving furniture in school? Well, you told me something that stuck. You said that you had confidence in me. So I decided to believe in myself as much as you did, and I think that's one of the reasons I chose to become an electrician. I also think it's also one of the reasons I decided to break off on my own and start my own company."

I felt proud of what he'd done with his life—and felt a sudden craving for a lilac mint.

The myth I believed:

Only the few are selected to win.

The reality I discovered:

If it is to be, it is up to me.

CHAPTER 10

I Decided I Was Smarter
Than I Thought I Was

─◈─

The myth I believed:

I know my limits; that's just the way it is.

Most people have a firm plan in mind when they turn in their job resignation after seventeen years of employment. I didn't have a firm plan, but I did know it was time. Seventeen years earlier, I'd graduated from college and rolled into the big city with less than a hundred dollars in my pocket. I didn't know the city at all, and had no friends living there, so I walked down a main drag looking at window signs that said, "Rooms for Let."

Within twenty minutes I snagged the perfect room. It was not only the cheapest accommodation I could find, but it was near a highrise landmark insurance building—so I could always find my way home if I got lost. I just had to look up for the tallest building in sight. The room was pretty shabby with a bare light bulb dangling from the ceiling and horsehair plaster hanging out of cracks in the walls. This place made my dorm room look like the Taj Mahal.

The ambiance was capped off by the bathroom, which I shared with three other people on my floor. I doubt if it was cleaned by anyone but me; it was a "hold your nose" experience at best. The only positive thing about the place was the absence of cockroaches—apparently, they have limits, too.

Perhaps the dismal digs made sense for a few months before I secured a teaching job; but after that, there was no excuse for staying there. Even so, I stayed for a year. Having come from very simple means, it was natural for me to just hunker down and save my money, rather than splurge on a nice apartment.

Now that I was out there in the world on my own, I guess I was haunted by my lifelong fear of being poor. That fear had long been fueled by my father's complaining about money issues and never having enough, what with a large family to feed on a very modest income.

Yes, my father's pay was enough to put a roof over our heads, food on the table, and clothes on our backs. But, ours was a no-frills lifestyle. When we asked about going to a drive-in movie or out for an ice cream treat, he almost always said we couldn't afford it. His lack of being able to provide more than the basics got him ranting about money at times.

So there I was, single, with no dependents, and making almost twice my dad's income. Yet I was living in my father's model of reality, not my own. In fact, when he came to visit me the first winter after graduation, he praised me for keeping the temperature low enough to freeze whale blubber and the lights dim enough to make a bat feel at home. I think he was more proud of me for living on the edge of poverty than he was when I graduated from college. In a strange way, this was the first time in my adult life that I was honoring him by following in his footsteps.

A year later, as I'd done in the past, I began inching away from my father's reality—this time, by allowing myself to enjoy the luxury of a tiny one-bedroom apartment (private bathroom included). The apartment was located in a different building; but just to keep things comfortable, I chose to live in the same *iffy* neighborhood so I could save a good percentage of each paycheck. I wasn't sure what I would inevitably use the money for, but it felt comfortable for me to save as much as possible every month. Over the next few years, I continued to make modest upgrades in apartment quality, but I never lived in a place that really reflected the increase in my earnings.

The upside of living so inexpensively was that I had several thousand dollars in my bank account when I decided to quit teaching and branch out on my own as an entrepreneur. My growing bank account was a great cushion, but it wasn't the catalyst for change. The real motivator was a student named Debbie who came up to my desk one day after class. In my sixteen years of teaching, no student had ever made such an interesting statement about herself or posed such a dynamic question.

"Mr. White, I've got a problem. I've got to decide that I'm smarter than I think I am. If I don't, I won't get into the school I want to attend next. How can I decide that I'm smarter that I think I am?"

Debbie was applying to a private high school that had a solid reputation for excellence. The school was prestigious, selective, and expensive. Debbie had her heart set on being accepted. Though she was certainly intelligent enough; she didn't act it, her grades didn't reflect it, and she knew it.

"Just how smart are you, Debbie?" I asked.

"Oh, average," she answered.

"How smart would you have to be to get into the school that you want to go to next?"

"Smarter than what I think I am right now. I know that for sure."

What fascinated me was that Debbie actually understood that she had the intelligence and capacity to get into the school. But she also knew that neither her grades nor her behavior demonstrated it. Furthermore, she knew why—she didn't think she was smart enough to aspire that high.

Talk about understanding your problems! This kid was totally in tune with her own mental barriers. She just needed someone to help her who believed in her more than she believed in herself. She sensed that I was such a person. She was right; I did believe she was smarter than she accepted about herself.

I told her she had to begin by simply reminding herself every day that she's smarter than she currently thinks she is. And she'd have to prove it to herself and to the world by acting that way.

"Say to yourself, 'I'm smarter than I think I am,' when you brush your teeth, when you get on the bus to come to school, when you enter each classroom," I advised. "And begin acting as though it is so. Join the study group with the smart kids instead of going to the gym to goof around during study period. Accept tutoring in the library after school, rather than hanging out on the sidewalk, smoking with your friends."

The upshot of this encounter was transformational. Debbie went to the library after school for tutoring. She joined a study group instead of hanging out during study period. Most remarkable, in a matter of months she turned her attitude about her intelligence around completely. Debbie was not only accepted to the academy, she was awarded a scholarship. Right there, Debbie helped me gain clarity about a question I'd pondered a few times over the past several years: if you have determination and know what you want, can you turn your life from monotony to creative living?

As so often happens when a teacher helps a student, lessons are learned and benefits occur on both sides of the desk. Debbie was inspired to decide in favor of herself by trusting that there was more to her than she'd previously believed. And Debbie's decision inspired me, ironically, to do something I'd been dreaming about for years—*leave* teaching and start my own business.

As I contemplated the possibility of exiting my profession, I remembered an article on entrepreneurship I'd read when I first began teaching. The article explained that being an entrepreneur is a matter of stepping out on your own, and being a "now" kind of person looking for new experiences. The article went on to say that going from "now" to new is one of the most rewarding experiences in a person's life.

The idea of being a "now" person and stepping out on my own was just a tease back then, one of those things I entertained as a fantasy. But the allure continued year after year. But me, an entrepreneur? How would that be possible if I wasn't sure I was smart enough to be a successful one, at that?

The following year, a month into my seventeenth year of teaching, when I learned that Debbie had definitely made her dream come true, I decided it was my turn to do my own version of what I advised Debbie to do: act as though I had what it takes to successfully start my own business. If Debbie had the courage to keep at it until she succeeded, it was time for me to prove that I had the same courage. When I gave my notice to quit a very secure job with a fabulous health and retirement plan, and tenure to boot, it was the appropriate and right thing to do. Enough yearning, more action. It was now or never.

Not surprisingly, when I announced my plans to leave teaching to be an entrepreneur, family, friends, and teaching colleagues all agreed that I was having a midlife crisis and should seek help. "Are you crazy? You've got it made. Don't blow it for some stupid dream."

It was tough, but I didn't waver. I turned in my resignation for the end of the school year right before the midwinter break. When I walked out of the principal's office, I felt dizzy. I heard a voice inside my head screaming, *Fool! What have you done?! Get back in there and tell him it was a mistake and beg for your job. You're a veteran teacher; he'll take you back. You love your students; you love teaching. Debbie didn't give up a great career and retirement plan to advance her dream; what's wrong with you?*

The voice screaming in my head was actually my father's voice. This was the second time in my life that I felt sure that I'd done something wrong—if looked at my choice through his eyes. The first time was when I ditched the opportunity to be in the fast lane to supervisor status at the factory, in exchange for a college education. Now, seventeen years later, as if I hadn't learned my lesson, I was on track for a getting promoted to the assistant principal position, and I was tossing *that* out as well.

Once again, I needed to muster up the courage to become the Bob White I wanted to be, rather than the Bob White whose life was laid out by others for me.

In spite of the firmness of my decision to leave teaching, it took me a couple of months to zero in on the kind of business I wanted to launch. I finally settled on real estate to be my avenue to success and riches, for two reasons. First, my research showed that more people get rich in real estate than in any other profession. Second, I'm a tangible kind of guy, and real estate is a tangible kind of career. It was also something I could jump into without needing any more degrees. As a plus, I really enjoyed learning about real estate; this was important, because I wanted to do something that genuinely intrigued me.

I was nervous, but excited, now that I knew the career I intended to launch. Shortly thereafter, I got my first glimpse of how much the universe really supports the person who is willing to commit to something unwaveringly.

One day, while walking home from the local grocery store, I came upon a book lying face down on the sidewalk. *What's this?* It looked brand new. I had to pick it up; who wouldn't? When I turned it over to examine the cover, to my amazement it read, *How To Succeed In Real Estate*. Succeed in real estate? This wasn't a coincidence, it was fate! I didn't find the book, the book found me. It was there because I'd made a firm commitment to pursue a successful career in real estate. I truly believed the causal connection back then, and still believe it today.

I tossed the book into the bag with my goods and continued to my apartment. After unloading the groceries, and putting the perishables in the refrigerator, I immediately flipped through the pages of the book. As I perused the chapters, my favorite quote from Goethe popped into my mind: "The moment one definitely commits oneself, then Providence moves, too. All sorts of things occur to help one that would never otherwise have occurred." My finding this book was a stellar example of Providence in action.

After inhaling a quick dinner, I began devouring *How to Succeed in Real Estate*. I took copious notes and began plotting my next move. No crib sheets necessary for this life test—I was going to do it straight up! I was so excited about this magical turn of events that I stayed up all night pouring through the contents of the book. As I completed the last chapter, I was ready to begin life anew. This was the moment when I could clearly see that if I marched straight toward my goals, without hesitation, I'd find that there is always more in life that is for me than against me.

The book confirmed that I'd made a great choice by committing to real estate. And the author went further by giving me a blueprint with action steps included. I had all I need to achieve my goals and beyond.

By the time I completed my final year of teaching in June, I'd read the book a dozen times. I immediately started right in with its prescription for real estate success, following it to the letter. I bought a three-family house as prescribed, lived on one floor, and covered the mortgage with rent from the other two apartments. Then I bought a second three-family house, and finally a third. This is where my savings account came in handy—I had enough in the bank to put ten percent down on the three houses I purchased over the next eighteen months.

I was doing everything right, according to the prescription. But two years after quitting my job, I was still making less than I did when I was a teacher. Although I could live on next to nothing, my savings had diminished considerably and the old money fears began to undermine my confidence.

One day, while wondering for the thousandth time if I'd made the right choice, I began to think I needed something to hasten my progress. That something eluded me, so I decided to seek out a mentor to help me fine tune my prescription for success.

There are successful real estate folks out there who would enjoy teaching me more if I approach them with the right enthusiasm, I thought. *It's time to get off my duff and find a mentor. After all, I'm not a getting any younger; if I'm going to accelerate my success-speed, the intelligent thing to do is to find a seasoned winner to advise me.*

So I thumbed through the *Yellow Pages* and called dozens of realtors and developers, asking if I could take them out to lunch and learn how I could hone my career in real estate. To my dismay, all of them politely declined my offer.

I tried the "dropping in" technique, making cold visits to real estate development company offices in the city and in surrounding communities. Same disappointing results. Fortunately, the more I heard, "No," the more deeply I vowed to find the right mentor. That worked well during the day, but at night I lay awake wondering if I made a mistake and would end up back in front of a chalkboard. There were definitely two of me—one optimistic and confident, the other pessimistic and worrying.

I made a conscious effort to side with the *me* that was optimistic, hoping that tenacity and a conviction to win would catapult this *me* to greater success. Sure enough, my persistence paid off. A few weeks later, while attending a fundraiser for a local clinic, I met Paul, a highly respected name in Boston real estate circles. We struck up a conversation and I told him my story, after which he handed me his business card. "Drop by my office tomorrow, Bob," he said. "Let's talk."

It turned out that Paul's office was a fifteen-minute walk from my house. How easy was that? I wasn't sure what specifically I was hoping to learn, but I made it a point to show up as the optimistic me that I wanted to be when I walked into his office the next day.

I told Paul that I quit teaching to get into real estate, and I explained my current business ventures and future aspirations. We spoke about the game of real estate for about an hour, and he gave a brief history of what he did to take his game from nothing to many millions. Paul sat silently for a moment then asked how old I was.

"Uh, low forties," I answered.

"I see," he said. "You're a little late to the game and, if you want to hit it big, you've got to get rid of the part of you that's afraid of making real money."

Paul's observation was scarily on target. After knowing me for just an hour, he saw my internal struggle and knew exactly what was holding me back. I didn't tell him I was from a small mill town, but he sensed it.

"You'll get eaten alive by architects, contractors, and anyone who can take a bite out of your bank account if they smell that nervous Nelly inside of you." Paul continued. "You need a guide through the jungle out there, and I'm up for a last safari. I'm in my seventies and winding down, Bob. I want a living legacy, not just a bunch of buildings. My boy's a doctor, and I'm proud of him. But he isn't interested in the real estate game. How about I teach you what I know and help you up your game? This could be fun."

I couldn't believe what I'd just heard. Everything he said resonated with me. In such a complex world, how could things be so simple?

"I'd be honored to be your student!" I enthusiastically responded.

Paul asked me where my office was located. I told him it was in an unused bedroom in my home, and he told me I could set up shop in a spare room of his office. He wanted me to be his assistant and to be a fly on the wall while he met with tradesmen, city officials, bankers, and other people essential to completing two development projects that he had going. He didn't put me on salary, but the education I got was worth far more than any paycheck he could have flipped my way.

After six months, Paul thought I was ready for a baptism by fire. He showed me a vacant lot for sale on the cheap and coached me through the whole process, from permit to construction, and finally the sale of six townhomes. Paul introduced me to his network of contractors and bankers, which gave me an incredible leg up on the process. Over the next two years, we had a ball together. He loved teaching, and I loved learning.

Now that I had a taste of success—real success, the optimistic *me* (which I believe is the real me) was winning the wrestling matches and pinning the pessimistic *me* quicker and quicker. It was time to up my game. I decided to jump into the condo conversion business—something that was relatively new back then. Since I had the necessary contractors to renovate old apartments, and a legal team to convert them to condos, why not give it a shot? I began making right decisions and taking effective action in what was a hot real estate market over the next four years. I watched my profit margin soar.

With the optimistic *me* showing up more and more in my life, I was not as tight with my money. I began spending a little more. In mid-February, when it was freezing in Boston, I decided to go to Maui where I had an opportunity to be part of a three-week Earthwatch expedition. I went there to be an assistant to a group of scientists who were studying whale behavior. I'd get to enjoy the new adventure, watch whales up close, and even learn something new. This worked out well because it was time for a break. But there was still that part of me that needed justification for spending the money. So in my mind, the trip was an educational, working vacation, rather than just a few weeks of lying around the beach drinking piña coladas.

The Maui trip had benefits beyond my wildest dreams. Not only did I love the adventure; but on that gorgeous island I met Kat, who is now my wife. The only challenge with this courtship was that when it was time for both of us to return home, Kat would fly to the West Coast where she lived, and I'd return to the East Coast. The solution was obvious. It came from my heart. I need new territory in which to work. How about setting up shop in California?

On the flight home to Boston, I retraced my steps from the mill town to the shores of Maui. It was quite a journey. And now I was going to take the biggest plunge of my life, all in the name of *love*. I reasoned that the California real estate market was always considered a gold rush, and it was time for me to mine for some gold out there. How delightful to realize that the pessimistic *me* was no longer the burden he once was.

Eighteen months later, after hundreds of phone calls to Kat, and to real estate brokers in her area, and after several short jaunts out to California, I was ready to act. I found a parcel of land and got permits to build twenty townhomes on it. Kat helped me to find the right builder; we met and we got along wonderfully. So my new West Coast real estate engine was in gear and steadily building up steam. I knew I was getting good when I came up with a winning name for the street I had to build through my first development: Bob White Lane.

Now I had projects going on both coasts. Back in Boston, my trusted crew of contractors, ranging from carpenters and masons to plumbers and electricians, were functioning effectively in my absence. All was well.

One particular carpenter in Boston, who did brilliant finished cabinet work, caught my attention. Stan was a master craftsman, but you wouldn't know it to look at him. He drove an old truck, rarely shaved, and his clothes smelled like they hadn't been washed for weeks. And yet, his work was impeccable.

After working with Stan for a year, I'd established enough rapport with him to ask about his background. He mentioned that he came from a family of nine kids, grew up in a low-income housing project, and was the only one in his family to rise above subsidized living. He said he took great pride in his work, and that he would never go back to depending on others. Here's the kicker: despite Stan's outward appearances, he was making more than $80,000 annually.

I asked Stan what he was doing with his money, and he said he was socking it away for a rainy day. My God, this was me just a decade earlier. I mentioned that I once thought that way and, as a result, developed very conservative spending habits to ensure I'd never be poor. I went on to explain that I overreacted and was, in fact, not spending *enough* money on myself. That in turn fueled my fear of poverty, which stopped me from ever trusting that I would experience prosperity.

Stan listened intently. I went on to tell him the Debbie story, and what it taught me—that I was far more capable of succeeding than I'd given myself credit for. He said he really appreciated the fact that I shared how I had the similar problems. He went on to say that he dreamed of someday owning a company with several carpenters working for him.

I assured him that as long as he sought excellence (which he very obviously did), and always did the best he could, then success was inevitable. "Maytag once had an ad that said 'excellence is an endangered species,'" I said. "Continue to seek excellence in what you do, and begin treating yourself with the respect you deserve, Stan, and your dream of owning a larger successful business can't help but become part of your reality. Never pretend you're something that you're not . . . and you're NOT a failure; you're already rich in a dozen different ways. Start treating yourself that way, and your future will reflect it. It seems to me that you have two Bobs wrestling inside. It's time for you to throw your support on the side of the optimistic you who loves to work and offer excellent service. These were all lessons that I'd learned over the past few years.

I made one final suggestion. "Dare to purchase a newer truck and buy some nice work clothes. Keep your truck and clothes as clean as your toolbox. You deserve it. Prove it to yourself. Dare to be your own best friend."

Stan listened, and took my advice. When I last heard from him, many years had passed; he was married, owned a lovely home in Georgia, had two handsome boys, and had more work than he could possibly take on.

You can live a life of hesitation, or you can live a life of inspiration. A life of inspiration requires believing in yourself today more than yesterday. Supporting this belief requires taking on more—the more you dare to do, the more you can do.

The myth I believed:

I know my limits; that's just the way it is.

The reality I discovered:

My limits are of my own making and are there for the breaking.

CHAPTER 11

The $50K Lie

◦─◈─◦

The myth I believed:

**A little greed and a lot of business savvy
is the recipe for financial prosperity.**

When I graduated from college and moved to the big city, I rarely went back home except to see my parents. There was one notable exception: the annual River Rat Race, which entailed paddling a canoe for five miles on Miller's River to the finish line in the neighboring town. I never won a River Rat Race, but I enjoyed the tradition, which began with a gut-busting pancake breakfast and ended with a blues band celebration in the back yard of Jake's Place, a tavern situated on the river where the race ended.

River Rat Races were always fun, and I looked forward to the spirit of friendly competition. So without hesitation, I signed up for yet another race and joined the hundreds of canoeists lined up on the riverbank with enough pancakes in their bellies to feed the crew of a full-scale armada.

Spring was technically upon us, but the air was cool and crisp, the water cold and choppy. I was happy to beach my canoe at the finish line and come ashore dry. That wasn't always the case for me in prior races; with so many canoeists jockeying for position, it's easy to wind up in the drink.

The town was awash in good vibes, and everyone was pumped for the big bash that would soon be starting at Jake's Place. The event would be replete with hotdogs, burgers, chips, beer, soft drinks, music, and good cheer—small town America at its best.

It was also great to mingle with the other River Rat racers who hailed from towns and cities throughout New England. About an hour into the festivities behind Jake's, I was approached by a well-groomed man in his late thirties. "Hello, Mr. White," he said, extending his hand. "I'm Tim Westly. Congrats on your canoeing today. Our mutual friend, Jake (the owner of the bar), thought you and I might have a common interest."

"Thanks, Tim. What's the common interest?" I asked, as

I reached out to accept his handshake. His grasp was strong without being excessively forceful. It communicated a confidence that matched the rest of his demeanor. But despite his good presence, I felt a twitch in my stomach that signaled me to be careful.

Tim went on to describe an exciting short-term, high-return investment he'd recently come across. I liked the combination of "short term" and "high return" in the same breath. I also liked the fact that Jake thought enough of this guy to send him my way, so I dismissed the warnings that were popping up on my internal radar screen.

The deal involved a liquor store in a neighboring town that was up for sale. According to Tim, it was already a lucrative business and could be purchased at a bargain basement price because the owner was retiring and wanted a quick sale to avoid any confrontation with his son, who had an alcohol problem, but nonetheless, wanted to take over the store.

Tim explained that the deal had all the ingredients for success today and expansion tomorrow, because it sat on over a half-acre of land and had a huge parking lot in the rear. Even sweeter, he went on, the deal came with a large barn that could be converted into a Laundromat, something the community very much needed. Tim was pushing all of the right buttons; he'd piqued my interest. So I donned my invisible business hat and set my canoeing mindset aside. I wanted to hear more. Tim went on to tell me that he'd already plunked down a $10,000 deposit and had a signed agreement to buy the store and business at a fixed price, but he needed another $50,000 to complete the purchase and sales agreement. The P&S agreement was necessary to apply for a liquor license. He assured me that transferring the license to his name would be a cinch. Now, it would be easy to secure the additional financing needed to acquire the business and complete the conversion of the barn into a Laundromat. "A no-brainer," he boasted.

His proposal was that I could be his partner in the project, and he'd buy me out for a cool $150,000 within a year. I'd triple my money, and all I had to do was come up with the initial $50,000. His calculations and knowledge were impressive—he really seemed to understand the opportunity at hand, although I was a bit put off by his overly confident style.

The idea of tripling my money in a year was certainly appealing. I'd never made that kind of money so easily, especially in such a short period of time. My real estate deals took eighteen to twenty-four months to bear fruit, and I was putting sixty hours a week into the projects. This was a different kind of business game, and I liked it.

A week later, after going in the liquor store, which was larger than I'd imagined, and looking over the business records of the current owner, which Tim provided, I set up an appointment with Tim at my Boston office. During the meeting, I went over everything, including the executed agreement between buyer and seller, with my name now included on it, and the application for a transfer of the liquor license in Tim's name. Everything was in order. We signed an agreement for our business relationship, and I gave him a check for $50,000 to seal the deal.

As I wrote the check, I looked at Tim and asked, "Is there anything else I should know that you're not telling me?" My inner voice was still giving me a big fat "NO" by causing a twitch in my stomach.

"Bob, you've got it all," he said, looking me straight in the eye. "This is the best deal I've ever done. I personally guarantee it's going to work out according to plan."

I handed Tim the check. We shook hands once again, and I went about my real estate business, leaving the liquor store deal to him. This was a busy time for me. I was completing a twenty-eight-unit condo conversion project and needed to bury myself in the details that would bring it over the finish line on time.

A week passed, and I'd spoken with Tim by phone a few times. He'd sent me a copy of the purchase and sales agreement signed by the owner after he handed over the $50,000 to the owner's attorney. All seemed on track; Tim had gotten a hearing date with the town council members to get approval of the liquor license transfer. The hearing, he said, was thirty days out. I called the town hall to verify the hearing date, and the secretary confirmed that it was on the calendar. About two weeks after that, the calls from Tim stopped, and I couldn't reach him.

Another week passed. No Tim. At that point, which was a week before the liquor license hearing, I was concerned. I called the town hall to see if there were any changes. Nope, everything was on schedule according to the secretary's calendar. I called the current owner of the liquor store to see if he'd heard from Tim lately. He said that he hadn't heard from Tim since he dropped out of the deal, losing the $10,000 deposit.

"What?! When did that happen?"

"Oh, I'd say a few weeks ago."

I immediately sprang into action. It didn't take more than an hour for me to realize that Tim had forged the owner's signature on the purchase and sales agreement and fled the scene with my $50,000.

At that point, anger and the desire for retribution took over my brain. I promised myself that this act of financial treason would not go unavenged. I hired a private investigator to assist in finding Tim so I could have him brought to justice.

With the help of the PI, I learned a few sobering things about my wayward business partner. First, he was a compulsive gambler with serious debt problems. Second, he had a felony record, which meant that by state law, he couldn't own a liquor license. And third, Tim had actually pulled the same $10,000 scheme in Connecticut a year earlier. The Connecticut caper involved a pizza parlor with a beer and wine license. His con worked there just as it did with me.

I contacted the current liquor store owner and explained the situation, hoping to convince him to return the $10,000 deposit so I could at least bring the loss down to $40,000. He was sympathetic to my plight, and said he was shocked when Tim dropped out of the deal. But he refused to return the down payment because of the opportunities he'd lost by taking it off the market for a couple of month. What he said next rocked me, "I'm surprised that a successful businessman like you got caught in this scheme. Never let greed make decisions for you."

Two months later, the PI found Tim's whereabouts. He'd just been evicted from an apartment in Miami, Florida, because of failure to pay rent. Apparently, Tim was broke again. "Most likely," the PI said, "your money was spent on the horses. This guy loved the racetrack." The PI went on to say that gambling was Tim's biggest curse, and he has some pretty scary people looking to collect on his gambling debts.

"Want a piece of advice, Mr. White? Let it go. You won't get a nickel out of this guy, and you'll spend twice what you already lost trying to get it back."

I grudgingly followed his advice and chalked it up to experience. In hindsight, I was foolish for not realizing that when Tim said the deal was a "no brainer" he was assuming I wouldn't use my brain to do a background check on him. And he was right. I missed some obvious initial cues. Cues like the fact that Tim gushed over my canoeing prowess when I actually finished toward the rear of the pack. Cues like the fact that Tim didn't actually have to know Jake to get his name; the sign over the tavern, "Jake's Place," was a pretty good clue! (Jake later told me he'd never heard of Tim.) Then there was the fact that my business success was a big part of the conversation in the small town in which I was born. Finally, I rolled into town in a fancy sports car, a rare sight to behold in my old neck of the woods. In short, I was a mark for a good con.

As much as I hated to lose the money, I took comfort in knowing I'd learned an important lesson that would pay huge dividends in the future: listen to my inner voice, and heed its warnings. An intelligent reaction, when presented with any important choice, is not only to ask, "How can I think clearly about this?" but also ask, "How does my stomach feel about this?"

A year after the liquor store fiasco, I met a fellow developer, Chris, and became fast friends with him. Over the course of the next year, we met every other Wednesday for a business lunch and exchanged tips on how to be more effective in the condo conversion market. We both left these lunches feeling pumped up and ready to take on the world.

During one lunch, Chris excitedly announced that he'd found a perfect plot of land in a great community, just right for building a five-townhome development. The lot had been sitting vacant for more than twenty years, and the family that owned it was willing to sell it for a fabulous price. He quickly moved to get it under agreement.

Everything said, "GO." The only problem was that his inner voice said, "NO!"

"What do you think I should do, Bob? I'm hearing a 'NO' from deep inside my gut."

I told him about the time that I ignored my inner voice, and it cost me $50,000. I advised him to listen to that voice above all else. "If your stomach is uncomfortable, slow down." I said. "The part of you that speaks from deep within can often see the unfolding film of your future. If you're sure it's that voice speaking, and not just a fear of failing, then heed its advice."

Chris thanked me and, after another week of pondering the deal, decided to let it go. A few months later when we met, he seemed annoyed with me. He explained that another developer bought the parcel, got a permit for five townhomes, and was in the process of digging so he could put in the foundation. "The developer will make an easy half mil when all is said and done," Chris said. He regretted taking my advice. He also said he should have ignored his nervous stomach and listened to the "go" signal from his head.

Another few months went by, and Chris was singing a very different tune—he was deeply thankful that he listened to me and heeded his inner voice's advice. He explained that when digging the foundation, the developer encountered two huge buried tanks. Apparently, there was a gas station on the site forty years ago. The station was long ago demolished, but the tanks were never removed and the lot remained vacant for more than twenty years. Everyone had forgotten about the dark secret lying buried under the site.

The Environmental Protection Agency was called in for inspection. They discovered that the tanks had leaked, causing soil contamination. The cost of soil cleaning was exorbitant, and the mountain of paperwork that would follow was daunting.

The developer found himself in court, fending off environmental complaints and suing the seller of the property. He eventually gave up and sold the site at a large loss to someone who was willing to take on the problems. Had Chris ignored the voice of truth—his inner voice—this would have become *his* nightmare.

—◈—

The myth I believed:

A little greed and a lot of business savvy are a recipe for financial prosperity.

The reality I discovered:

When it comes to money, greed skews judgment, while the inner voice offers clarity.

CHAPTER 12

The $3M Shakeup

⬦

The myth I believed:

What happens in my world determines how I feel.

Big Sur. Malibu. Santa Cruz. Monterey. Sonoma. California was a dream world to me. I'd never experienced such
natural beauty. And the people! They couldn't be more different from buttoned-down Boston. When I arrived, everything
in California felt new and right, it was flashing a bright "green
light' for me. While courting Kat and replicating the real estate
development strategy I'd honed on the East Coast, I bought a
lovely oceanfront home on Monterey Bay, a place to relax and
rejoice in how well life was unfolding.

California was primed for mega real estate growth. Every town hall was pro-growth and pro-development; so getting
building permits, variances, and local support was easy if you did
your presentation properly. The formula was to offer quality and
build with environmental consciousness. Within a few years, I
had a couple of West Coast development successes to my name.

I was feeling pretty confident and ready to graduate to the
big leagues. Why limit myself to a twenty-townhome development? Why not a larger scale residential development? So I
managed to attract the perfect partners, and we purchased a
seven-acre lot with the aim of building fifty-two single family
homes with backyards, and fences around them. After coming up with a sizeable down payment (much of the money being mine), we secured a multimillion-dollar construction loan.
Over the next eighteen months, as we obtained the necessary
permits, we assembled a dynamic construction team. Things
were moving nicely. We began paving the roads and pouring
foundations. Everything was a go!

Perhaps I was too enthusiastic and confident. Had I paid
more attention to where I was developing my project, the name
of the street leading to my development—San Andreas Road—
might have triggered a warning light. Yes, that's "San Andreas"
as in the "San Andreas Fault."

The engineer I hired did make a joke about the proximity of the site to the fault line, but I didn't want to hear anything negative about the project—certainly not about some crummy old tectonic plates. Besides, engineers and geologists are just like weathermen—they get off on scaring you with *any* possibility of a catastrophe, no matter how remote the likelihood of it happening.

Well, on October 17, 1989, at 5:04 p.m. Pacific time, Mother Nature decided to give me a fifteen-second lesson on probability. At that exact time, I was on one of my frequent flights from Boston to California when the pilot announced that we were being diverted to Dallas. News soon buzzed through the cabin—a major earthquake had struck northern California. The airports in San Francisco and San Jose were closed, and Governor George Deukmejian had declared a state of emergency.

The quake measured 6.9 to 7.1 on the Richter scale, the biggest since the infamous earthquake of 1906 (7.7 to 7.9), which devastated the city of San Francisco and much of Northern California. Dozens of people were dead from the recent quake, and thousands were injured. The major highways were closed. No one knew how long air travel to the Coast would be disrupted. Fourteen hours later, I found myself back in Boston.

Of course, my first concern was for Kat, and there was no way to get hold of her. When my phone rang at one o'clock in the morning, it was Kat telling me she was all right. She said that the aftershocks were constantly rattling things, and the epicenter was in Nisene Marks State Park in Santa Cruz, which was close to the development site. She couldn't tell me much more than that. I assumed that things had gotten jostled a bit, but that we'd be back in business within a few weeks.

When I was finally able to fly back to California, several days later, I saw Kat and met with my partners who had grave looks on their faces.

"Is it that bad?" I asked.

After a brief silence, one of the principles, Ken, said, "Let's put it this way, Bob . . . Godzilla couldn't have done a better wrecking job. You can't get near the development to see the damage because the area is blocked off for safety reason. It will probably cost more to repair than the project's total worth."

I wanted to see for myself, but no one was allowed within a quarter mile of the surrounding area, except for the disaster officials, engineers, and geologists. It wasn't until later in the week that I was able to get close enough to appreciate the extent of the damage. The foundations really *did* look like they were ripped apart by a prehistoric creature. Eighteen months of work and 3.5 million dollars invested had simply vaporized in a matter of seconds.

At least I have insurance, I told myself in consolation. But while the front of my mind was processing the astounding damage, something in the back of my mind was gnawing at me about the insurance coverage—something wasn't right. That something was the exclusionary clause in the policy that we purchased, stating that the earthquake insurance only kicked in when the tie downs—steel X-frame beams that enable a building to withstand violent tremors—were in place. Sadly, we'd not gotten to that point yet.

After absorbing the insurance aftershock, I began panicking about the bank loan. Surely, I thought, the bank will forgive the debt—this wasn't my fault, it was an act of nature. There must be an "act of nature" clause in the agreement with the bank; that's only reasonable.

I made an appointment with Karen, the bank officer who

worked with us to secure the original loan. She was already on the case. "I'm so sorry you lost all that money, Rob," she said in a sympathetic, but banker-like, voice. It was the banker-like tone that sent a ripple up my spine.

"Um, you mean the million dollars I put in?"

"No, your million, plus the amount of money you've drawn from the construction loan for the past year. So adding in the down payment, that's a multimillion-dollar loss."

Karen just looked at me, unflinching. I asked if I could use a phone in a private office so I could call Wayne, my attorney.

"Wayne, tell me there's a clause. Is there?"

"Sorry, Rob, no Santa Claus, no escape clause," Wayne said, trying to lighten things up. "

"There's nothing funny about that," I retorted.

When I returned to my house, Kat took one look at me and knew that the quake was just a prelude—my emotional tremors were just getting going. She had no idea about the seismic events about to play out in my head.

Over the next several months, I frequently traveled back and forth between Boston and California. During that time, I went through my own version of Elizabeth Kubler-Ross's five phases of grief.

First there was denial. I kept telling myself that there's got to be something I'm missing here that will make it all right. Every day, I'd wait for the moment when I'd pinch myself and say, "Ah ha, here's the piece to the puzzle that will save the project. That moment never came, because there was no missing piece. My resentment and refusal to accept the truth was contaminating my ability to move on with my life.

Next, I felt like a victim. I talked endlessly about how I'd gotten sucker-punched by life. Feeling angry with reality and sorry for myself, I began to wonder if all of this "positive thinking stuff" really worked. Was this a reality check, and I flunked. Was all of my success a grand tease, a run up to the moment when the rug would be pulled out from under me, leaving me on my mill-town butt with nothing but the clothes on my back and shoes on my feet?

From the victim stage, I oscillated between anger and rage. "I'm suing the bank for giving me a loan on risky property. I'm suing the lawyer for not telling me that there's no earthquake clause that guarantees my money back. I'm suing the engineer who inspected the parcel of land and didn't twist my arm into building somewhere safer. I'm suing the county for giving me the permits. I'm suing all the Californians who should have warned me. I'm suing God—all of them!"

The fourth phase was deep resignation. It's over. I'm going back to Boston, selling everything and closing my real estate business, and then I'll see if I can get a substitute teaching job. If that doesn't work, there's always the factory in my home-town; maybe they're looking for a good janitor.

Finally, I slipped into depression, marked by a feeling of helplessness. There's a definite connection between feeling helpless and bad manners. I became downright rude. My spirit was reduced to the psychic equivalent of the rubble left after the quake. So with nothing but a huge hole in the ground and an equivalent hole in my wallet, I moped around the house as I cleaned up business matters in California.

A month into the helplessness phase, I sat on the deck, overlooking the Pacific Ocean, and watched a remarkable scene unfold in front of me. Against the backdrop of a brilliant blue sky, a family of dolphins leapt out of the water, intermingling with surfers and swimmers. I decided to take a stroll on the beach. As I approached the stretch where people were surf-ing, my eyes focused on a woman who was standing on the beach, teaching her son how to ride the waves. The mom was in her thirties and had the archetypal trim California body and blonde hair. Her son, also blond and trim, was maybe twelve years old. Both were clad in neoprene wet suits with bright-blue panels on the sides. The boy ran into the surf and stood up on his board.

"Put your arms out higher, honey," she shouted. "Use them for balance!"

Just as it looked like he'd gotten the hang of it, the boy's triumphant stance was dashed by the wave that he was riding, sending him tumbling over the surfboard and into the ocean. Mom dove in to make sure her child was okay, and the two made their way back to the beach. The boy sat down, sputtering and crying.

"I'm not going back out there again," he blurted out amidst his sniffles.

"Hey," she said as she sat down and held his chin toward her own face. "Are you going to let one wave decide for you if you're surfing days are over? If you get on a board, you're going to wipe out. That's part of the thrill. And that's when you have to decide to get back on the board and try again. What's it gonna be for you?"

With that, the boy got up, grabbed his board, and ran into the ocean once again. He fell a few times, but clearly he'd learned an incredible lesson that day.

And so did I. His mother's words echoed in my head, although I said it a little differently. "Am I going to let one shake of the earth decide if my real estate career is over?" Wow, that's exactly what I was doing. *No way!*

As I walked back to the house, I asked myself at least a dozen times, "Rob, are you going to let one shake of the earth decide your future in real estate for you?"

Within the next five minutes, I realized that what had happened to me was not a cosmic joke, but a cosmic *test*. Yep, the game of life had thrown me a tricky curve ball. I took the bait and struck out. But now it was my choice. I had the option of slinking into the dugout or stepping back up to the plate for another round at bat.

When I got to the house, I went straight for the telephone. "I'm back!" I hollered with glee to one of my old Boston real estate brokers. "Find me a deal. We're revving up the old Bob White Development Machine. I'm getting back in the game . . . I'm gonna stop whining and start winning again!"

I'd once read that a right attitude is always the first right move for right future action. I used to say it often. I'd forgotten that, and it took a California surfer mom to remind me.

About a year later, immersed in an exciting real estate project in Boston, I met Darrel as I cut through the Boston Commons on my way to a meeting. Darrel was a guitarist and blues singer who was once popular with the local club circuit. He'd fallen out of favor and onto tough times, living in subsidized housing and spending most of his days in the park, and evenings in local pubs where he talked about the good old days. New gigs were few and far between for him, especially as he slid deeper into the bottle.

I struck up a conversation with Darrel out of the blue, and could see, in the deep lines of his face, a hard life. Over the next couple of months I made it a habit to go through the commons so I might bump into him. I found him interesting, even though our conversations were typically one-sided; he repeated the same story about the "knock-out punch that life handed him" when he foolishly let a famous blues singer steal one of his songs.

I decided to try and break the cycle by telling him my

earthquake story and the lesson I learned from the California surfer mom. I didn't really expect it to take root in his mind, but the words that came out of his mouth when I finished surprised me. "Are you saying the dark and low part of me has taken over my life, and all I know how to do is ache?"

"Wow, where did that profound insight come from?" I asked him.

"It's a line in one of my songs," Darrel responded, "Maybe I need to heed the advice of my counselor."

Darrell went on to tell me that he was seeing a counselor, and the counselor said that he'd sung too many blues songs in his lifetime—now he was living the songs he'd sung. He asked if I thought that could be the case.

"Well, there might be something to it," I replied. "If there's one thing I learned for sure from last year's earthquake experience, it's this: No matter how much you give in to a whining mind, it's never enough." I then asked him, "What if you give guitar lessons and spend more time making a little money doing what you love to do rather than spending so much time in the pub and the park?"

The next statement out of his mouth sounded like perfect lyrics to a new song in him: "If you want to find heaven, you've got to send a prayer there and not to hell." He then asked me if I'd lend him a few hundred bucks to get started.

I told him that a right attitude is a right prayer, and agreed to make him the loan if he promised to use the money wisely. It was a great investment. He's back on his feet, giving guitar lessons and playing a few local gigs every now and then.

By helping him, Darrel helped me to further understand that recognizing an inspiring truth is not enough. You've got to get off your duff and take action to prove that new truth is valid. Who are you proving it to anyway? YOU!

If you ponder a great start but don't take action, your dreams remain dreams. Take action, and your dreams can take flight.

⟡

The myth I believed:

What happens in my world determines how I feel.

The reality I discovered:

How I respond to what happens in my world determines how I feel.

CHAPTER 13

Flying Dangerously

—◈—

The myth I believed:

I get trapped into doing things that I don't want to do.

I 've long had a hobby of collecting quotes that I've read in various books and magazines. I find them often to be the energy boost I need for motivating me to solve a problem or put action into my plan. One quote that really hit home was from the historian Arnold Toynbee: "The only thing we learn from history is that we learn nothing from history." I thought about that quote many times in the months following my post-quake reintroduction to the real estate world. I was determined to prove the idea wrong in terms of my own history.

Another quote I saved was one my Uncle Fred loved saying when an event didn't have a happy ending for someone in the family. Fred was quick to chime in with his optimistic tone, "Every new beginning comes from some other beginning's end," and then he'd add, "Seneca said that."

My father always chimed in, "Seneca . . . that's a pretty strange name; don't know if I trust his judgment."

Well, after the earthquake loss in California, I was determined not only to prove Toynbee false, but to prove Seneca's statement true—no fault lines or other hidden traps would stop me from advancing.

I jumped back into the game of real estate by purchasing a parcel of land that was considered unbuildable in a vibrant neighborhood of Boston. With a little hard work and a lot of smart thinking, I attained the zoning variance needed to build eleven attached townhomes. Getting the variance was a challenge, but being completely involved in the project helped me disconnect the noisy chatter in my mind that had me feeling unsure of my future.

As my real estate business began to flourish once again, I began craving new experiences unrelated to my business life. I began thinking of a quote attributed to Helen Keller: "Life is either a daring adventure or nothing."

I wanted my life to be a daring adventure. So I attended a weeklong workshop where I became certified as a fire-walk instructor. Afterward, I held my own fire-walks for corporations and for the general public.

At other workshops I learned how to break through half-inch boards with my bare hands and how to calm my mind while pushing a sterilized pin through the flesh of my hand so it only felt like a simple pinch. I learned how to sit peacefully in a one-hundred-plus degree sweat lodge with fifteen others—all of us stuffed in there like sardines. I even learned how to jump out of an airplane with a parachute on (the only way to do it.)

If it raised my adrenalin, I wanted it. And on the occasion of one of my birthdays, I gleefully accepted my wife's offer for an experience sure to get my heart thumping: a wild stunt ride in a biplane. Her offer literally came out of the blue. She knew how much I enjoyed sitting on the deck, watching the local biplanes pilot do their unofficial air shows over the Pacific Ocean, with the loops and flips and other daredevil maneuvers. One beautiful red plane often caught my eye as it went through wild antics in the air. The pilot did a few daring stunts, and then took the plane into a swirling downward plunge toward the water. Just when it looked like disaster was imminent, he yanked back on the stick and the plane climbed to safety. His death-defying act of courage threw me into overdrive.

"I've gotta do that," I said to Kat. She cocked her head and smiled, knowing that there was one big problem with my declaration: I was prone to motion sickness, and I didn't like it when I wasn't in control. And certainly this experience would test both of these tendencies.

"Really, flyboy?" she asked, "Why don't we go to the local airport and sign up this weekend. That'll be my birthday present to you."

The next morning, we hopped in the car and drove to a small airport a few miles from our home. A sign on the fence listed the ride rates: $150 for twenty minutes, $300 for an hour. Nearby was the red plane I saw the day before. It was a magnificent piece of machinery, one that conjured up images of dashing young aviators who took to the skies and engaged in life-and-death duels without breaking a bead of sweat. Tom Cruise, *Top Gun* types of men with nerves of steel. Real men who thrived on danger, just like me. But as I looked at the open cockpit and the guy-wires connected to the wings, my bravado began to wane. "Um, twenty minutes will be fine—this time," I said.

The pilot explained that he'd been doing this for forty years. "I always put safety first," he said, handing me a helmet, goggles, and a leather jacket. He strapped me into the seat directly behind his. I felt like I was being buckled into a kiddie seat in the rear of a passenger car.

We took off, way more abruptly than I'd expected. The roar of the engine was deafening, and the wind felt like a brick wall. When my stomach settled down after a few minutes, I began to enjoy the incredible panoramic view. There was my house! And there was Kat, who'd driven home to watch the show from the cliff.

Upon seeing her, my cockiness crept back in. We weren't doing anything really scary or death defying, I thought, just a little wing tipping. So I tapped the pilot on the shoulder and yelled as loud as I could, "Hey, do some of those flips, you know, those twirly things!"

"Are you sure?" he yelled back.

"Oh, for God's sake, what do you think, I'm a sissy?" I hollered.

With that, he let the nose drop, and we started spinning down toward the ocean like we were going to crash. Immediately, my inner voice started screaming at me, "Are you nuts? What have you done? Forty years without an accident—this guy's due for one! Why did you provoke him? Look at the odds—we're doomed!"

The engine noise muffled my inner howling as we continued our plunge into the drink. Just when I was certain we were going to be shark bait, he swooped up and leveled off. We floated along, smooth as could be, as if nothing had happened. Within minutes, we'd landed and taxied to the space by the parking lot. The pilot hopped out with a big grin on his face. "Great ride!" he enthused, reaching over to unbuckle my harness. "Did you have fun?"

I was about to tell him that he got a little too close to the ocean, when I realized that he gave me exactly what I asked for. No, it wasn't his fault; it was my wife's fault; why would she take me seriously? And giving me this experience as a birthday gift, really!

Of course, I knew this wasn't the truth, but I had to laugh at how quick I was at trying to shirk responsibility for my choice in the matter. How strange it was to realize that I pretend to know myself so well, but am so quick to blame the world if things don't work out as I expected.

A couple of years after my biplane flight, Kat and I were in Tucson, Arizona, where I was building a "spec house" to sell in a hot housing market. We went there to spend some time with the contractor I'd hired, Brian, and his wife Susan. We'd had many phone calls, and I liked his style. Why not mix a little pleasure with business? Kat suggested that we round out the trip with a helicopter ride into the Grand Canyon.

Susan thought the idea sounded great, so she and Kat got on the phone and made arrangements. When we arrived at the helicopter pad, Matt the pilot greeted us with a big, broad smile, and proceeded to tell us that he had thousands of hours of flying experience. A Vietnam vet and former combat pilot, Matt had flown through gunfire numerous times, and began telling Kat and Susan all about it. It was like Brian and I weren't even there. He also spoke at length about the thrill he got from maneuvering through the Grand Canyon. He promised us a "real" helicopter ride *if* our stomachs could take it.

"Wow, we'd love it," Kat and Susan chimed in together."

Oh yeah," I mumbled, "really great." I wondered if Brian noticed my lack of enthusiasm, but my curiosity vanished when I saw the look on his face.

When we got to the helicopters, we were offered a choice. We could all go together in an A-Star helicopter that carries five passengers, or we could go two at a time in a smaller Hughes chopper. Matt highly recommended the smaller helicopter for maximum thrills. Kat and Susan instantly opted for the smaller helicopter; Brian and I nodded in silence.

"Which couple wants to go first?" Matt asked.

"Uh, ladies before gentlemen!" I blurted out, trying to be chivalrous. "Why don't you gals go together, because you're so excited. We'll go next."

Brian added, "Yeah, great idea."

Our wives hesitatingly agreed, noting that we were acting a bit out of character. Minutes later, they were buckled in and airborne with excited smiles on their faces.

The roar of the engine and blades gave way to a palpable silence, which I broke by admitting, "There's no way I'm going up in that thing with that guy."

"You got that one right," Brian echoed.

I went on to explain that I got nervous about flying in smaller craft since my biplane ride over the Pacific Ocean. Not white-knuckle nervous, but upset enough to want to avoid small planes if possible. Brian said he hated flying in any plane, and getting into a helicopter was about as appealing as under-going a root canal without anesthetic.

We debated our next move and decided that when our wives landed, we'd just tell the truth—the chopper flight wasn't our cup of tea. Thirty minutes later, Matt, Kat, and Susan returned, and we were ready to fess up.

Matt gave us a look, sized us up, and said, "I find this a lot with couples," he said in an understanding tone. "One wants to go and the other only says 'yes' to be accommodating. Well, I sense this with you guys. Your wives got the thrill of their lives, and the good news is that I see I have several customers waiting to take a ride if you'd prefer not to go."

So the whole event turned out to be a triple win. The women loved it. Matt didn't care because he had other customers waiting, and Brian and I got off Scot-free. Even better, Kat and Karen didn't mention the incident—they were too busy recalling the thrill of skimming along the Canyon.

Six months later, I was in back Tucson to sell the spec house. Brian and I went out for dinner to celebrate the successful business transaction. During the course of the conversation, the Grand Canyon excursion came up. Brian said that the issue really was about control; he explained that he was a guy who started with nothing and worked his way up, and he got there by being in control of his life. I knew exactly what he meant—Brian and I lived in the same psychological village when it came to control issues. And being in a helicopter with a gonzo guy in control was not very inviting.

My conversation with Brian helped both of us notice the sly stunts we play on ourselves throughout our lives. We concluded that noticing inner stunts helps avoid unnecessary turbulence while navigating through life.

The myth I believed:

I get trapped into doing things I don't want to do.

The reality I discovered:

Look within—that's where the trapping begins.

CHAPTER 14

Life in the Fast Lane

❖

The myth I believed:

Sometimes insisting you know is the speed lane to victory.

One night while channel surfing, I stumbled across a Formula One car racing event at the Laguna Seca Raceway, known for being one of the best Formula One race courses in the world. Something about the deep growl of the engine and the sleekness of the car, grabbed my attention. The idea of me zipping around a raceway at top speed revved my engine and got me up off my feet. It was time for a high energy fix, and this opportunity was only forty miles away.

I placed a call to Laguna Seca the next day, and was excited when I learned that Formula One driving classes were available. Daydreaming is part of future planning. I began daydreaming about flying around the Laguna Seca racetrack at top speed. This was meant to be, especially given that the track was so close to my home.

I asked my wife Kat if she'd like to try it; and to my surprise, an enthusiastic "yes" popped out of her mouth before I even finished the sentence. I don't know why her response surprised me—Kat always likes a good challenge.

"Great, I'll give you some pointers," I said, feeling that this was really a guy thing.

"Wow, thanks, hon," Kat replied.

We called and signed up for the next available class, which was a week later. The morning of the class, we drove out to the raceway. During the trip, when not chatting with Kat, I fantasized about leading the pack around the course and getting high praise for my driving prowess. "Kat would surely be impressed," I figured.

When we arrived, I was awed by the track as we drove by it, and then we found the parking lot, adjacent to a very plain looking two-story building. The first floor was where drivers fitted up with a properly sized fireproof suit and helmet. The second floor was where the classrooms were located. My heart sank when I walked into the classroom and I saw the blackboard and desks. Boring! Unfortunately, class time was mandatory if we wanted to drive. I didn't realize it at the time, but I had taken on the attitude of some of my students from prior teaching years: "Who needs this?"

Kat's eyes focused attentively on the blackboard and ears focused on the instructor. She took in every word about the aerodynamics and mechanics of driving. She even took notes. The other students in the room, mainly middle-aged men, were also paying close attention to the teacher. As well they should, I figured; they probably didn't possess the natural driving skills I had. I was staring at the racecar sitting on the track. I had a clear shot of it from my window view. *C'mon, it's just a car*, I kept thinking. *Let's get out there and drive.*

The instructor droned on and on, and my frustration increased. I also had a startling and scary thought: *Was I this boring when I taught?* My assessment of this guy's teaching style distracted me for another hour, at which time the class was finally complete. Kathy, along with all the other novices who needed the course, was finally prepared for action.

After a quick lunch, we headed to the first floor where we decked out for the big event. The instructor made sure we were properly fitted with the right racing attire, and then escorted us to the raceway where the cars were parked. Kat's car was white; mine was metallic blue. "*What magnificent, awe-inspiring machines,*" I thought to myself. "*So shiny and smooth; they look like they could defy gravity.*"

We climbed into the driver's seats of our respective cars, and I found myself staring at a half-moon-shaped steering wheel and a Spartan dashboard equipped with a speedometer, tachometer, temperature gauge, and fuel gauge. Pretty simple. I was startled back into the moment when the instructor shouted, "Cinch your harness tight." He barked out the same order several times. "Adjust your seat so your knees and elbows have a slight bend." When he felt certain that we'd all followed orders, he then went over the key points he'd covered in the morning session.

"Remember, the car stables more when it's going faster. You have to resist the temptation to break when you go into a curve. If you break, you'll wind up in the gravel trap. As I explained in class, look where you want to go, your body will take care of the rest. If you stare at where you *don't* want to go, that's exactly where you'll end up."

It's an intelligent moment when you realize that you've been given a good piece of advice, and you heed it. This wasn't an intelligent moment for me because I didn't feel I needed such advice. I didn't remember the instructor mentioning anything about *not* looking where you don't want to go. What's the big deal?

"Get ready—when you push the starter button, you won't be able to hear me."

We hit our starter buttons, and the engines roared to life. Power surged through the car. The sound was deafening and my whole body vibrated as if it were a loose part that needed to be bolted onto the frame. Just like on television, a guy with a checkered flag came out in front of the cars. With a swift wave of the cloth, we took off. I threw the car into gear and felt my body slam back into the seat. I can only describe the feeling I had as a pure adrenalin surge. I suddenly understood why the instructors refer to the cars as "beasts"—animals that crave speed; part car, part mythical creature, the responsiveness defied the imagination. I'd owned Porsches and other sports cars, but the Formula One made them seem like M47 Patton tanks.

The first car out front was the "pacer," a professional driver who sets the speed. We started off on a straightaway, and it was easy. However, when we came to the first corner I stared right at where I did *not* want to go, which was over the gravel embankment, and I instinctively went for the brakes. Well, I didn't go into the gravel, but I did find myself falling behind the other cars.

Crap, I thought. *I got myself a lemon. This car's not performing as it's supposed to.*

"Wait a minute," I immediately said to myself, "What did the instructor say? Look where I WANT to go, NOT at the corner!"

Ah, I'M the instructor now. So, instruct yourself intelligently.

As I got my bearing once again, I couldn't help but notice that Kat was way ahead of me, right behind the pacer car. Huh? She sailed through the next corner like a pro. Clearly, she trusted her natural driving skills, and she learned what she needed to know from the classroom instructions.

The second corner was a little better for me, and I improved with each corner after that. Yes, I was teachable if I wanted to be. By the third lap around the track, I found myself focusing on where I wanted to go by slowing down my mind so I could speed up the racecar. No more nervous chatter; I simply laser-focused by pre-setting my eyes on where I wanted the car to be next.

After three laps, we made a pit stop. We got out to stretch, and I looked at my racing colleagues, decked out in their white driving suits and helmets with face shields. I chuckled to myself when I noted that we looked more like a troupe of astronauts than fledgling racecar drivers. It felt good to be part of this elite group.

The next three laps were even more exhilarating. We went faster and I flew around the corners without hesitation. On the last corner, one of the few things I remembered from the class flashed into my mind: "Keep in mind that one successful corner leads to another and another—it starts a positive chain reaction."

On the way home, Kat and I were exuberant. How strange; I wanted to do something that would give me a new thrill, and what I drove away with was much more than that—some great tips to use in my everyday affairs: look where you want to go in life, not at where you don't want to go . . . Don't hesitate at the corners; excuses will slow down your progress . . . One successful corner can lead to another and result in a positive chain reaction . . . Listen for the thumping sounds in your journey through life—they mean you're drifting out of the lane and heading for a crash . . . and, perhaps the biggest of them all . . . life gives you many opportunities to learn how to navigate through the world safely; there's no better teacher than experience. But, eventually *you* must become your own instructor if you plan to win.

I thought a lot about the concepts that I'd learned at Laguna Seca, and how they applied to my life. An unexpected opportunity to teach them came up several months later when I was I was approached by an inner city youth organization in Boston that was seeking funding to support a teen bowling league. My money would be earmarked for the "Gutter Busters" team. I gladly paid for the bowling shoes and T-shirts they needed, and I enjoyed attending practices during the season. It gave me great satisfaction to see the kids having fun and focusing on healthy competition. Unfortunately, the Gutter Busters were missing the "busters" part—most of the balls wound up in the gutter. In fact, they threw more gutter balls than any other team in the league.

After one particular practice session, the Gutter Busters were feeling down, so I bought them ice cream and sat across from the team captain, a tall young man named Sam.

"I think you guys might want to stop looking at the gutters and pay more attention to where you want the ball to go," I said.

Sam nodded.

I explained how I'd learned that lesson at the raceway. The next game, every time Sam got up to bowl, he'd say aloud, "Look at the pins."

The other team members soon picked up on Sam's words and began chanting it to one another, "Look at the pins."

The chant became the team mantra and had an immediate impact on both morale and performance. By the end of the season, the Gutter Busters were indeed living up to their namesake and went from last, out of seven teams, to third place.

I attended the end-of-season banquet. When Sam accepted the third-place trophy, he thanked the city organizers, thanked the coaches, and thanked me for the shoes and shirts. "But mostly," he said, "I want to thank Mr. White for the chant that took us from seventh to third—look at the pins. He added that we went from seventh place to third when we stopped looking at the gutters.

Rhadi, another one of the kids, approached me during the dinner to tell me he was using the chant to get better grades in school. He told me that he now says to himself, "Look at an A" before he takes an exam. His plan was to bring his grades up from C. I left the dinner feeling that perhaps I'd helped these kids navigate a little better though their own lives. It's amazing what can happen if we just focus our hearts and minds on where we want to go. Simple idea, powerful results.

The myth I believed:

Sometimes insisting you know is the speed lane to victory.

The reality I discovered:

When my ego declines, I open my mind; and now I find the quickest path to the finish line.

CHAPTER 15

Running with the Bulls

—◆—

The myth I believed:

When feeling upset, it's normal to act distressed.

After a hard day at work, there's nothing I like more than meeting up with friends and going to the local Mexican restaurant for some homemade chips and salsa. During a chips and salsa evening one hot July eve, I was intrigued by a poster hanging on the restaurant wall: 200 people running through the streets of Pamplona, Spain, ahead of a herd of supercharged bulls. It was a photo of the annual running of the bulls, an event known all around the world. When I got home, I did a little reading and learned that, though there were numerous bull runs in other cities around the world, Pamplona was the place to be, if you wanted to do it right.

My wanderlust overtook me. I was immediately convinced that running with the bulls was part of my destiny. I wanted to be part of a tradition that began more than 500 years ago, born of a simple logistical need to get the bulls to the marketplace. The running was also popularized by Ernest Hemingway in his novel, *The Sun Also Rises*, one of my favorite books in college.

Here's how the modern bull run version works: at the start of the event, a fireworks rocket is launched, indicating that the bulls are about to be released from their pen. A second rocket indicates that the bulls are on the loose. The bulls, agitated by the pyrotechnics, charge down the street in a section of town that's been cordoned off for the event. They run toward the bullring, about 1,000 yards down the road, where they're corralled and stabled. The idea is to get them stoked for the main bullfighting events to take place later that afternoon. A third rocket is an "all clear" signal, meaning that the bulls are in lockdown and secured.

The goal for the human runners is to stay ahead of the bulls and arrive at the bullring area without getting trampled, then scale a five-foot fence without getting gored. It takes the bulls four or five minutes to get to the bullring, so you just need to be a little faster than a bull to make it there in one piece. Plus, you get a head start!

I didn't want to procrastinate with my destiny, so the following year I arrived in Pamplona a few days before the event and did some practice runs. My times were good; I knew that I was ready for the actual event. I was ready on *many* levels: mental, physical, and emotional. Most important, I made certain that I was properly dressed for the occasion; nothing was more critical in a bull run than being dressed for success. The runners traditionally wore white paints and a white shirt, with a red scarf around their waists. Some wore red bandanas around their necks, and the ones who really wanted to amp things up wore bright-red shirts. I wanted to roll with the best of them, especially if I was to be caught on television. So before leaving the States, I swung by Rodeo Drive in Beverly Hills, California, and purchased an outfit befitting any modern American bull runner who had deluded himself into believing he would lead the pack and be a national hero in Pamplona.

My well-coordinated ensemble included designer white beach trousers, a red leather belt, a limited edition white silk shirt, and a pair of handcrafted red-and-white leather running shoes. When I looked in the full-length mirror, I was pretty impressed. I saw a guy who was tanned, buffed, impeccably dressed, and ready for action.

The night before the event, I learned from the locals that smart runners carry a newspaper with them. If a bull is bearing down on you, the smart thing to do is toss the pages of the newspaper into the air to distract him. I was also told that I'd get the maximum adrenalin rush if I didn't take off when the first rocket exploded overhead. "You'll be too far ahead of the bulls, and you'll miss the challenge," advised one villager. Apparently, the real runners waited until the bulls nearly caught up—then they ran like hell.

I was also cautioned about the biggest danger of all, which is the people running ahead of me. If they trip and I trip over them, I'll provide excellent shielding as the bulls use me for a doormat. My mind was not put at ease by their blasé attitude, or the fact that none of the fifteen documented deaths related to the event resulted from the bull's hoofs—in each case the horns were the culprits.

With this knowledge in mind, I went to bed early, but barely slept a wink. At the crack of dawn, I initiated a critical visual checklist in front of the full-length mirror on the closet door:

Shirt, pressed and buttoned. Check.

Red leather belt, cinched to my waist—looking athletic and trim. Check.

White beach trousers, pressed and spotless, perfectly creased. Check.

Leather shoes, laced, with tightly balanced knots. Check.

My bull running clothes were flawless. All that remained was a head check. I looked back at the mirror.

Every hair in place. Check.

Teeth brushed and white. Check.

I was now ready to engage the herd and headed down to the festival. When the first rocket exploded, at around 8:00 a.m., I ran like hell, forgetting that if I waited, the challenge feels greater and the thrill of the run heightens. Within moments, I realized I was suddenly part of a human wave. My emotions ranged from pure thrill to sheer fear. Mostly though, I was driven by the primordial instinct to survive. It was fight or flight, and I left the fight to the matadors, who were part of the next act. A few people in front of me fell, and I jumped over them as if they were hurdles on a track. This was every runner for himself!

As I threw myself over the fence to safety at the bullring, I felt someone grab my shirt, using me as a booster to help himself traverse the fence. I was totally winded and in a euphoric state, but I now felt angry. Yes, I was still alive, and I would go down in history as another brave soul who understood the need to keep the fires of tradition alive in the modern world. But the nerve of this the panicky coward who ripped my silk bull-runner shirt? I'd never find another one like it; and even if I did, it still wouldn't be the original. I'd planned on wearing my victory shirt when I got home. It would be perfect for barbecues and beach parties: "What a great shirt, Bob. Where'd you get it?" And then I'd begin my heroic tale of "running with the bulls" in Pamplona, Spain.

To add to the disaster, my red-and-white leather running shoes were ruined; caked in mud and scuffed from toe to heel. They looked like I'd found them in a dumpster. I cursed aloud. " No shirt, no shoes, no proof—who's going to believe me when I talk about this death-defying adventure? If I wore the remnants of my outfit, they'd assume I'd gone to a mud wrestling competition in Waco, Texas, and then rode a mechanical bull.

In the midst of my mental tantrum, I looked over at the culprit who ripped my shirt, to give him an angry glance that would surely teach him a lesson! What did I see? A bare-chested guy in his sixties laughing and smiling gleefully, loving the moment he'd just experienced. Right there, it became clear to me that I was missing the point. I just experienced a triumphant moment of beauty. Rather than celebrate it, I was choosing to get angry about trivial things.

I think back about that bull running experience and my misplaced priorities when I catch myself getting upset about foolish things these days. If I have my health, wonderful relationships, happiness, and success, have I not already sailed over the arena wall? The rest is just bull.

A couple of years later, I was tidying up my yard when I got a call from a college friend, John. He'd left a sales career a few years earlier to start his own business, but things didn't work out as he hoped. We got together a couple of times a year to go to a Boston Red Sox baseball game and just catch up on what's happening. He told me he wanted to make a big splash at our next college reunion. Knowing I wasn't going to attend, he asked if he could borrow my Porsche Cabriolet convertible for the day. He asked reluctantly because he knew I kept the car in mint condition, looking as if it just rolled off the showroom floor.

"Okay," I said, "Have a great time. Just bring it back in one piece."

"I'll be careful, Rob. Thanks!" John said with great conviction.

The following Saturday, the day of the reunion, the phone rang. I picked up the phone, and before I finished the "lo" in "hello," John blurted out, "Oh my God, I've wrecked your car! I know the insurance will cover the repair, but it won't be the same car. It was perfect. There's no way I can pay you to replace it. What can I do to make it up?"

The first thing that flashed through my mind was to chide him. "Damn it, John." Pre-Pamplona, my nostrils would have been flaring like an angry bull, and I'd have charged anything red.

But I calmly said, "John, you're okay, right? And no one got hurt?"

"I'm fine. Everyone's fine. While backing up, I hit the gas pedal instead of the break and plowed into an oak tree. Even the oak tree is fine."

I immediately said, "You backed into one of Mr. Lampkin's oak trees? I'm really glad that the oak tree is fine. Otherwise, we'd have to answer to *Mister* Lampkin."

This struck a responsive chord because John was one of Mr. Lampkin's landscaping crew members, along with me, back in the sixties, when the famed rose bush massacre occurred at UMass.

We both began laughing so hard that we couldn't talk. When John finally caught his breath, he admitted that he'd spent far too much energy all of his life trying to impress others, and it was time to grow up. "My God, I ruined your car. Worse, I almost ruined one of Mr. Lampkin's oak trees, just to impress old classmates. When am I going to learn?" We began laughing uncontrollably again.

John thanked me for being a great friend and helping him learn an important lesson. I decided that when we got together later, I'd tell him that the real teacher here had four legs and two horns. And I'd reveal a lesson I'd learned from overreacting to my shirt being ripped. Imagine destroying a beautiful, long-term relationship by overreacting to a dent in my Porsche. I knew he'd get a kick out of it.

The myth I believed:

When feeling upset, it's normal to act distressed.

The reality I discovered:

Feeling upset sometimes may be unavoidable, but acting distressed is always optional.

CHAPTER 16

It's Just Me

❖

The myth I believed:

Impress others—get the applause of the world.

"**Y**ou've got to go straight for the center of the board, and you've got to follow through, or you'll sting the palm of your hand," I warned the volunteer from the audience who was about to break a half-inch pine board with his bare hand.

"Breathe deep. That's right. Envision your hand thrusting easily through the board. Now *feeeel* it happening; that's right, *feeeel* it, *feeeel* your hand thrusting through the board. Not TO the board, but THROUGH the board, and then strike!" I roared.

Like magic, the board would snap in half, clean as a whistle if the volunteer did as instructed. He would then stare at the board in amazement, as if he'd just been responsible for the parting of the sea.

I had it all planned out.

"You've just proven something important to yourself," I'd say. "If you can break a board with nothing but your bare palm, you can easily break through the limiting beliefs that stop you from achieving those dreams that are important to you. Aim directly for the goal that inspires you, and thrust forward, just like you did with the board. All obstacles will fall away."

The audience always went nuts—they loved it.

So went the motivational speaking gigs I started doing after reading hundreds of self-help books, meeting tens of well-known self-help gurus, and deciding it was time for me to jump back into the teaching gig, but now as a motivational speaker. I had a knack for delivering messages with passion. I could move the audience. My new hobby was a lot of fun, with benefits. One week I'd fly to Chicago, the next to San Francisco. I was having the time of my life. Within a year, I connected with one of the bigger real estate companies, and they hired me to fly all over the country to energize their brokers.

The real opportunity came when I was invited to give my presentation at the company's annual convention in Las Vegas.

There were 15,000 people expected to attend. *Here's my big chance to become a star,* I fantasized. *If I pull this off, I'll get a standing ovation and then who knows what's next—maybe Hollywood's my next stop—the movies!*

I considered this a greater thrill than skydiving and race-car driving combined. I could hear the applauding audience in my head grow louder until it was like rolling thunder across the plains of my consciousness.

The day of the convention finally arrived, and I could hardly contain my excitement. Before I left my hotel room to perform the gig of my life, I stood in front of the full-length mirror.

Shoes, shined. Check.

Trousers and shirt, neatly pressed. Check.

Tie, properly knotted. Check.

Teeth, pearly white. Check.

Skin, healthy and tanned (healthy tans were "in" back then). Check.

Hair, perfect. Check.

I took the elevator to the hotel mezzanine and walked across the breezeway to the main event hall. The show kicked off with the corporate heavies doing their *blah-blah* and *rah-rah* stuff. When it was finally my time on stage, I walked up confidently and told the large audience that one of them was going to achieve something as magical as anything they'd ever seen in Vegas.

After a ten-minute warm-up motivational speech, the crowd was ready. I explained that I wanted someone to come up and smash through a half-inch pine board. I held the board high so everyone could see it was solid and without cracks. A camera displayed the stage on a huge screen behind me, so even folks in the rear had a close-up view. I'd glanced at myself on the screen for one last "All set to go." Check! "Lookin' good."

I took about thirty seconds, looking around at the audience, and asked for a volunteer who'd like to try to split the board. A number of hands shot up across the auditorium. I chose someone who seemed like an unlikely candidate to succeed: a woman in her fifties who was dressed to impress, with enough heavy jewelry to stock a department store. She didn't look like the athletic type—you wouldn't have thought she could break a toothpick let alone a half-inch board. Perfect.

There's no way a standing ovation isn't coming, I thought to myself.

The volunteer came up on stage, at which point I had her introduce herself to the audience. I asked a few questions so we'd know a little about her—where she was from, about her family, what she liked best about her work, and so on.

I asked, "Are you ready?"

She said, "Yes," and the performance began. I began to explain what she needed to do if she intended to successfully break through the board. "Stand straight. Breathe deeply. Focus your attention of going *through* the board, not just *to* the board."

I went on to say how this could be a defining moment for her, "After this experience, there's no obstacle you'll consider unbreakable; imagine applying this kind of determination to your real estate career!"

She was psyched; I could feel it. I, too, began to feel a rush of adrenalin. The air was filled with tension. And heat—the lights were beating on the stage like the sun over the Sahara Desert. Unfortunately, the convention center's air conditioning system wasn't performing as it should, and a bead of perspiration began forming along my forehead. I picked up the board, and with a flurry of dramatics snapped my head high as I commanded her to strike.

The thrust of my head changed everything. Her hand never came near the board, because she never moved a muscle in her body. She was too dumbstruck by what had just transpired: the revealing of a deep, dark secret that I'd been harboring for years.

Despite the fact that I made a point of looking fit and successful, the perfect hair that I'd just admired in the mirror an hour earlier had just fallen off my head. Yup, I wore a wig, which was now lying on the stage, looking like a cat curled at my feet.

I looked down at the wig in a state of panic, then over at the woman standing there. She was staring at me. I turned around and looked up at the giant screen behind me and was stunned to find that the videographer wasn't missing a thing. And then I looked out at the 30,000 eyes staring at me. The silence in the room was deafening, magnified by the supersized image of my glistening head on the jumbo screen.

The truth was out. I was not the dashing dude I pretended to be, decked out in my hand-tailored custom clothes, handcrafted shoes, and a Rolex Oyster watch. I was a middle-aged guy, who spent a lot of money and energy over the past decade trying so hard *not* to look bald. Just a few years back, while in the heyday of my restaurant ventures, my hair-hat had even passed the acid test—I was profiled in the *Boston's Most Eligible Bachelor Directory*—a local publication that included a photo showing my thick, wavy brown locks.

So there I stood with my shiny, bald head, like Captain Picard, from *Star Trek: the Next Generation*, poised on the bridge of the Enterprise. Rather than gazing at strange new worlds where no one had ever gone before, I was staring at a sea of people who stared right back at me.

There are no words capable of expressing what I felt at the moment. So I did what one in panic mode does when confronted with a life-threatening situation: take flight and look for an escape route. The red glowing exit signs at the far end of the auditorium caught my eye, but I'd have to run past fifteen thousand people to get there. No good. Then I had a brainstorm. Fire exit laws would no doubt require exit doors behind the curtains at the back of the stage. So I slowly put down the board and did a Michael Jackson moonwalk to the back of the stage where I slipped through the opening in the curtains.

My plan was to dash out the rear exit door, skulk to my hotel room, pack, and take a taxi straight to the airport. Unfortunately, things didn't go as planned.

There was no exit door behind the curtain. Even worse, the curtain didn't extend all the way to the floor, so everyone could see my feet as I frantically scurried right and left behind the curtain, looking for an escape hatch. I stood there, behind the curtain, screaming to myself, *Beam me up, Scotty!*

It was over. There was only one thing left to do: surrender.

In that instant, I had a flashback. *Oh my God!* In horror, I remembered how petty I was so long ago when I met Joe the barber. I remembered thinking I'd walk around with a bag over my head if I were that bald. *Well, where's my bag?*

I walked to the center of the curtains, turned so I was facing the audience on the other side, with my feet pointing out from underneath the fabric. Of course, even those in the back row got a close up view, because the cameraman never stopped rolling. No way the videographer was going to miss this once-in-a-lifetime performance. Lucky for me, the Internet and video sharing hadn't been invented yet.

Slowly, I separated the curtains, mustered all the dignity I could find, and walked to the front of the stage. I picked up the microphone I'd dropped during my escape attempt, kicked the wig off the stage and onto the floor, and stood there looking at the audience. I turned to look at myself on the jumbo screen one more time. I turned and looked at the audience once again. The room was still dead silent. I calmly spoke six words: "This is who I really am."

I looked around the room for a few seconds.

I heard clapping from somewhere in the back. One of "us"—a bald guy—stood up and was applauding. Within a few seconds, another man, with a full head of hair (I think it was his hair), also stood up and began applauding. Then a woman stood up. And then, spontaneously, *everyone* jumped up and applauded. *This* was my standing ovation! The entire audience clapped and cheered. A tremendous truth was revealed that day: nothing is better than being authentic.

I'd gone from hero to zero and back in the span of a few minutes, as I discovered and conveyed a lesson more valuable than the one I intended to teach. Yes, the ability to break through seemingly insurmountable barriers is critical to being effective in life, but being true to yourself trumps everything else. And you'll never truly feel like you've succeeded if you aren't comfortable in your own skin.

I flew home feeling just "okay" about my bald head. I'd left the wig on the floor by the stage; but I was still feeling a bit nervous about how I would deal with family, friends, and business colleagues. Of course, they'd notice and probably remark, "Bob, what the hell happened to you?"

I needed a response that wouldn't leave me bumbling. I didn't want to get defensive, and I didn't want to be rude. I decided I'd say, "What happened is: I'm wigless and loving it. By the way, I prefer to be called Rob from now on. My new nickname will remind me of my new identity, which is the real me—authentic and free. I'd love it if you'd help me with this."

My father could hardly contain himself when he saw me. He belly laughed and said, "Isn't it a little early for Halloween? You look like Mr. Clean!"

So I told my father that I was wigless and loving it, and I was changing my name to Rob to remind me to accept myself as I am.

Dad smiled and said, "I used to call you Robbie when you were little. It'll be real easy to start calling you Rob."

It was a proud moment when I gathered the last of the wigs neatly stored on the hooks in my clothes closet and donated them to a local joke and costume shop. Pretty soon, the world was used to bald Rob.

Not long after I stopped wearing a wig, I met a young real estate broker named Michael. He was likable, but after introducing himself as Michael J. Vanderbilt, he always sighed and said, "Yes, I am a descendent of *the* Cornelius Vanderbilt, also known as 'the Commodore.'"

His introduction gave the impression that he felt as though he offered no value to the world without his "pedigree." What he didn't understand was that he turned off a lot of people with his affectation.

After a couple of business dealings with him, I felt we had a solid enough relationship that I might be able to help him realize his own worth without any regard to his lineage. I told him about my speaking gig with the wig, and how my whole identity had somehow been caught up with having a thick head of hair.

Without prompting, Michael looked at me and asked if I thought he made too much of his last name. He admitted that a few friends had suggested he drop the pompous dialogue and just be himself.

"Try it," I said, "See what it's like. You can even take it a step further; if someone asks if you're a descendant of Cornelius, say you don't know. Then see if they walk away and want nothing to do with you."

"I hope they don't walk away," he said with a laugh. "How am I going to sell them a home if they won't talk to me?"

Michael was, in fact, a good salesperson and quite charming when you got to know him. Several months later, he told me that things were going great for him on many fronts. He said he was able to establish better rapport with his clients as soon as he let go of the idea that being a Vanderbilt meant something. On top of that, he met the love of his life. Apparently, just being himself was more than good enough. He added an insight that he'd had that I've never forgotten. I added it to my "favorite quotes" notebook: "A free man is free, Rob, because at some point in his life he's willing to stop hiding and be himself."

The myth I believed

Impress others—get the applause of the world.

The reality I discovered:

Impress myself. The greatest reward is inner applause.

CHAPTER 17

The Squawk Heard
Round the World

The myth I believed:

If I see it—it's true.

During my fifties, it seemed like I spent as much time in the air as I did on the ground, constantly on the move for my real estate business, motivational speaking gigs, and kick-back relax vacations. During one trip from Tampa to Boston, I was traveling with my wife Kat, and Shakespeare, a twenty-inch, vocal, fluorescent green-and-yellow Amazon parrot.

"Shaky," who I call my friend of thirty years now, often accompanied me on personal excursions and has probably logged more flight time inside commercial aircraft than most parrots log in the big blue sky. It was actually easy to travel with a parrot back then; security was loose. Nowadays, they pass the wand over him and could possibly bump him from the flight for carrying a pointed beak.

We arrived an hour early at Tampa International Airport, and I was hungry. Kat had the good sense to eat breakfast before we left. It wouldn't be long before Shaky would start lodging complaints about his empty belly, too—I'd forgotten to bring his favorite meal, sunflower seeds. So, I set out to forage for the two of us in the nearby food court.

Now I have nothing against Tampa International Airport, but I can say that it was not parrot-conscious, even though there are a lot of parrots in Florida. I walked around the food court and couldn't find a single seed for sale anywhere, except those on the sesame buns. So I had to make do with what was available. I bought an egg salad sandwich and a bag of tortilla chips that I could share with Shaky. To cap off the elegant repast, I purchase a three-pack of Hostess mini-chocolate cupcakes with a squiggle of decorative frosting on top and crème filling in the center. I savored those pastries; I couldn't wait to sink my teeth into each one. They so reminded me of Aunt Theresa's delicious cupcakes from my childhood years.

With the food acquisition part of the mission complete,

the next task was to secure a place to eat. I did a recon and found a potential target at two o'clock: a table in the corner of the food court, with three empty chairs. The only obstacle was that it was occupied by a small, prim and proper-looking woman who was sitting in the fourth chair, drinking a cup of tea. I asked if we could join her. Even before she could reply, I began taking over the space, depositing our bags and bird on the chairs around the table, and my recent food purchases on top.

Amidst my clanging about and my parrot squawking for food, I heard "Why, yes," in a lovely British accent.

I did hesitate for a moment, wondering if the British had any rules about eating lunch with a very vocal parrot. *Oh what the heck, she'll get over it.* Yes, the table was small, but we could make it work as long as she stayed within her 9.5 percent allotted space.

I opened the top of Shakespeare's carrier so I could give him a chip (escape is not part of his personality). As I unwrapped my sandwich and readied myself to dive into the feast before me, I began engaging our captive audience in what I was sure to be exciting conversation, hoping she wouldn't notice what just happened to her tranquil, private environment.

I tore open the chips, grabbed one, and handed it to Shaky while telling her about the alligators we saw in the swamps. Who wouldn't be interested in that?

Shaky extended his beak and snatched the chip from my fingers with surgical precision. The feeding maneuvers were moving along like clockwork.

While I ate my sandwich, gabbing away with my mouth full, I gave Shakespeare another chip to keep him quiet (he only eats around the edges and squawks when he wants another one).

Kat decided to get involved and politely introduced us to the British woman, who cheerfully told us her name, "Philippa."

Philippa began telling Kat that she was on her first visit to America and couldn't wait to see more parts of the country. She was curious about where we hailed from.

Kat told her that we had houses on both coasts, and that she was born in California and I was from Massachusetts.

My impromptu lunch-mission strategy was going swimmingly well, I thought, until it was time for dessert. I looked around for my package of mini cupcakes and was surprised to see them on the other side of the table, next to Philippa. In my haste, I must have shoved them over to her side of the table when we first sat down. I stretched over, grabbed the cupcakes and pulled the package to my side of the table. I proceeded to rip open the cellophane, and remove one of the three chocolate frosted treats. As I bit into it, I was amazed to watch Philippa reach over and take one of my cupcakes and nibble away while smiling at me.

What the heck? Taxation without representation was one thing; but, eating a person's cupcakes without permission, that's quite another. *The Brits are a bold people, aren't they?* I asked myself. *Maybe it's some strange custom they have. But, whatever the reason, that's not how we do it on this side of the Atlantic.*

At the risk of starting an international incident, I grabbed the package with the remaining cupcake and placed it in my lap. I was quiet as I finished the first cupcake and proceeded to inhale the second one whole. While I was busy stuffing my face, Philippa continued to chat with Kat about California as she polished off the cupcake she stole from me. Kat and Philippa were getting along famously, which confused me all the more.

I was tempted to interrupt their conversation with an etiquette lesson or a stern reprimand, but I decided I'd be bigger than that. I hoped Kat would notice and surely be proud of me for my restraint.

About five minutes later, Philippa gathered her things, mentioned what a pretty parrot Shakespeare was, and bid us a good trip. As she walked by me, she gave me a pleasant tap on the shoulder as she said good-bye.

Once she was out of earshot, I said to Kat, "Did you see that? She swiped one of my cupcakes and didn't even apologize!"

"Actually," Kat said, "considering the circumstance, I thought she was pretty decent about the whole thing. You, on the other hand, Robert, could use a manners check."

"What are you talking about? She's a cupcake thief!" I wailed.

"Really, Rob?" Kat went on to explain that I had reached across the table, snatched Philippa's cupcakes, and shoved one in my mouth.

"Philippa's? Those were my cupcakes," I insisted.

"Nope," she said, shaking her head. "When you sat down, your cupcakes fell on the floor. I picked them up and placed them on your travel bag, right by your feet. I thought you saw me do it, but you were so busy taking over the table. Look, they're right here!"

I looked down at my travel bag. There was a full, unopened package of Hostess mini-cupcakes in their pristine state.

It took me a few moments to accept reality. And after several attempts to come up with some other answer, I had no choice but to accept the fact that I was the unpolished party here. If anything, Philippa was wonderfully gracious for tolerating my barbaric behavior. Not only did she put up with my barging in and taking over 90.5 percent of her space, but she accepted my brazen act of opening and eating two of her three mini-cupcakes. There was no doubt about it, she wasn't a common cupcake thief. I was!

Kat offered an explanation that made me feel even more foolish. "Perhaps Philippa now thinks it is customary in America to share one's food when you share a table."

In turn, she may have thought I'd be insulted if she didn't allow me to make a pig of myself.

That explanation worked for me.

I wish I could meet my UK table mate again so I could thank her for the lesson she taught me with her polite response to my outrageous action: there is no act more offensive than to be rude and boorish, and no greater act of kindness than to simply let it be. Philippa displayed three wonderful character qualities that I now work to make part of my personality: cheerfulness in the face of rudeness, tolerance in the face of discourtesy, and forgiveness in the face of intrusiveness. And most of all, she gave me the opportunity to notice that I cannot see reality when I unyieldingly insist that I already know what's true. If I had another chance to meet Philippa, I'd apologize and hand her a full box of chocolate cupcakes with squiggly white frosting on top and luscious crème on the inside.

Not a month had passed after the cupcake caper when I was at a friend's office having a business chat. A week earlier, he'd insisted that he'd returned my autographed hard copy of Stephen Covey's book, *The 7 habits of Highly Effective People*.

I'd insisted that he hadn't, but I dropped the matter. It wasn't worth bickering about any longer.

During our conversation, I happened to glance up at his bookshelf, and there, not three feet away, sat my book! *What?* I thought. I had the urge to point at the book and prove that he was wrong about returning it. But then Philippa came to mind.

As I was leaving his office, I cheerfully said, "I'm just going to grab my book on the way out."

His jaw dropped when he saw me reach over and pull it from the shelf. Nothing more was said, and I felt good about how I handled it. No scolding. No "I told you so." Just quietly taking my book and letting the matter be.

I have experienced many times since then that I don't always have to prove I'm right to win at the game of life.

⟡

The myth I believed:

If I see it—it's true.

The reality I discovered:

If I look beyond what I insist is true— I often find something new.

CHAPTER 18

The Guru in the Red Dress

—◇—

The myth I believed:

Those who get the most toys, and attention, experience life at its richest.

Over the next few years I found myself in a holding pattern. My real estate ventures were humming along, and I was enjoying a comfortable living. But I was getting stale. I wanted to challenge myself. I wanted to do something that would leverage my skills and knowledge, and would be fun, too. The restaurant business seemed like the perfect possibility.

Why a restaurant? Well, some folks open an eatery because they love food and they love cooking food. Others choose the restaurant profession because they're people persons and love the hospitality business. And still others will open a restaurant because they think they will make a lot of money while having a lot of fun.

My reason for opening Devon on the Commons in the late eighties was a combination of all of the above with the exception of loving to cook food. I liked partying, I liked the glamour of being a host at my own restaurant, and I liked knowing that when I showed up, my seat was waiting for me at the corner of the bar (sort of like Norm, at Cheers, except he didn't own the bar). Of course, the cherry on top was that I liked the idea of making money in a different way than my usual real estate route. As you can see, my reasons for opening a restaurant weren't profound, which was a reflection of where I was with my spiritual growth and development. Not far.

I opened Devon with two partners. We got along famously and were truly excited about the venture. We purchased a building in a great location, with the intention of developing an unusual three-floor restaurant that included a pub/cafe on the ground floor, a lunch/bistro on the second floor, and an upscale, white napkin, martini-with-a-twist restaurant on the third floor.

The pub/cafe would serve up Cajun fare, while the lunch bistro would offer a variety of American dishes. The top floor restaurant would feature nouveau cuisine, marked by elegant presentation and higher prices.

The only thing we hadn't figured out was the name. So we all sat down in the shell of the building (it wasn't renovated yet), and began brainstorming. Since the building was located across from the Boston Common we kicked around names like "Paul Revere on the Common" and "Grill on the Common." But nothing really struck a chord. Then I remembered a conversation I'd had with Charlie, the history teacher at the school where I once taught years before. While chatting in the teacher's lounge, Charlie mentioned that in the late 1700s there were cattle grazing on the Boston Common. The breed of cattle, called Devon cattle, was nicknamed "Red Rubies" for its juicy red meat. When I suggested "Devon on the Common" and explained the name, we knew we had a winner. Danny, our chef would be thrilled, because beef was one of his specialties, and every successful restaurant has some kind of signature house dish.

Our restaurant had a name and a specialty, and would soon ready to open for business. The first year did surprisingly well, given how tricky restaurants can be, especially for new owners who don't have restaurant experience under their belts. Fortunately, the three of us were very optimistic, and our attitudes were soaring. I believe that's what got us through the first several trying months.

About a year into my new venture as a restaurateur, Joan, a friend who taught elementary school, asked if she could bring her second graders to Devon for a field trip.

"Absolutely!" I exclaimed. "I'd love to give them the inside scoop on what it takes to run a restaurant."

Although I'd left the education field years before, apparently I was still a teacher at heart. *Perhaps this was an opportunity to motivate a new generation of entrepreneurs*, I thought. *Yes, it would be a great learning day for them.*

When that learning day arrived, a school bus carrying nineteen children pulled up in front of Devon. I was dressed for success and ready to impress. As the kids piled out of the bus, I felt excitement and joy radiating from their beautiful, enthusiastic smiles.

Joan and I escorted the children into the restaurant, which wasn't opening its doors to the public for a few hours. This made it easy to give them the deluxe tour without disturbing any patrons. The plan was to take the class through the different levels of Devon and explain how each operated. It sounded like a great idea. But, as we all know, even the best ideas can quickly go awry.

The first indication that my expectations were a bit high came when a boy whose nametag said "Timmy" held his nose and screamed "pee-you!" as we entered the ground-floor pub.

"What's the matter?" I asked.

"Smells like my grandfather's yucky basement," he answered.

"Oh, this is where we serve delicious Cajun food. That's food like they make in New Orleans, down in Louisiana. Do you know where that is?"

"It still smells like Grandpa's yucky basement," he repeated.

"Ya, it stinks in here," another boy chimed in.

That's not how I'd envisioned the script playing out—the children were supposed to be in awe. The first response to the pub was not a five star review.

We gradually made our way to the third floor, by which time the kids were showing all the signs of utter boredom. But that changed quickly when we hit the kitchen. Their eyes lit up like the shiny pots, pans, and cooking utensils hanging from the ceiling. For some reason, they were drawn to the polished oversized stainless steel Wolf stove and Sub-Zero refrigerator. Apparently, they'd never seen anything that large and shiny before. My chef, Danny, took great pride in making sure the kitchen was as spotless as an operating room, and he was beaming from ear to ear. His jaw dropped as he eyeballed the fingerprints that were beginning to adorn the appliances.

After Danny gave a brief kitchen tour, we escorted the kids into the third-floor dining room, where they had a surprise waiting for them: fresh-baked chocolate chip cookies and milk. I'm not sure what planet my brain was on when I planned the field trip, but I had the tables set with our best linen tablecloths and napkins. Within seconds, the tablecloths looked like Jackson Pollock paintings done exclusively in earth tones.

Now it was my turn to inspire them. I began speaking about the value of hard work and how it leads to success in life. I was so busy yammering away that it took me awhile to notice that the kids were all looking out the window at a large gray squirrel on a tree branch. The squirrel was staring at the cookies.

Well, I thought, *at least the baked goods are a hit.*

I quickly asked if anyone had any questions for me, and was delighted to see one young girl in pigtails waving her hand frantically and squirming in her seat.

Aha! I thought to myself, *there's at least one future entrepreneur in our midst here.*

So I jumped on the opportunity and said, "Hi, Margaret," (looking at her nametag), "What's your question?"

"Margaret pushed her chair back, stood up, flared her dress, and asked exuberantly, "Do you like my new red dress?"

WOW! The question may as well have been about some arcane element of quantum physics. It was a complete pattern interrupt.

Wait a minute, I thought, *what are we talking about here, my restaurant or your new red dress?* In that instant, I recognized that I'd been hit over the head with a powerful lesson by an unlikely teacher. It was in that moment that I realized: everyone doesn't live in a universe in which everything orbits around me.

Margaret's life revolved around her jubilance over her presence in the world, symbolized by the new red dress she was wearing. Her child's-eye view of the world as "me, me, me," is exactly what it should be—it's only natural as a youngster finds her voice in the world. But, there's a point where you're supposed to grow and develop beyond that me-focused world. It's called maturity. It's that moment when you understand that if the world is going to work, it must be "thee and me," not "me, me, me." It took Margaret, with her red dress question, to shake me awake to the fact that I'd not yet made the transition from "me, me, me," to "thee and me."

When I snapped back to the moment, I responded, "Yes, I do, Margaret. Your dress is beautiful, and you look very pretty in it."

Joan looked at her watch and announced that it was time for the class to leave, because the bus was waiting outside the front door. Joan asked each child to take a brief moment to share what he or she liked best about the field trip. Most agreed that the big hits were the cookies, the giant shiny stove and re- frigerator, and the squirrel. I didn't get any votes. I thanked the class for coming; and they all thanked me, in unison, as Joan had instructed them to do.

I walked outside with Joan and stood by as she counted heads to make sure all the children loaded onto the bus. From her seat by the window, Margaret waved to me. I waved back as I pondered the lesson she taught me.

Later that day, I realized that this was indeed a big learn- ing day, but not for the kids—for me. There was much more for me to learn from this experience. Margaret's question was more than a "kids say the darnedest things" incident to be shared at a barbecue while cooking hotdogs. Her question was a wonder- fully disruptive moment—not just because it was so off topic, but because it interrupted my usual way of seeing things. She forced me to look at myself in a way that I'd only glimpsed at before—my need to be the center of attention was driving a lot of my action.

As the day went on, I sensed that I had to drive this lesson deeper into my consciousness if it was to have power in my life. But I wasn't quite sure how to do that. I arrived home at around 11:30 p.m. that evening, flipped on the television, flopped down onto the couch, and dozed off. The next thing I knew, my eyes popped open and it was two o'clock in the morning. I was thinking about my cleaning staff.

I'd always paid my people well and tried to be a mentor as much as a boss, but now I understood that every one of my employees, from the cleanup crew that works in the wee hours of the morning to the chef, had their own world that's was important to them as mine was to me. And yet, they took the time, every day, to help me realize my dream of being a successful restaurateur by taking pride in their work. They showed up on time and did a great job taking care of business.

I knew what I had to do. I had to go back to the restaurant and personally thank my cleanup crew for being an important part of the operation of the restaurant. I put on a pair of jeans and a T-shirt, jumped back into my car, and headed back to the restaurant.

When I arrived, the five members of the cleanup crew were busily doing their jobs. They were shocked to see me, especially dressed so casually. I acknowledged each of them for the contribution they made to the restaurant's success, then grabbed a bucket and mop and worked beside them for the next hour. They were visibly pleased that the owner actually came back in the wee hours of the morning to offer heartfelt appreciation for their work. I'm not so sure they were pleased with my cleaning skills; clearly they were getting a lot more done in a shorter amount of time.

By going back to the restaurant that night, I moved the Margaret experience from being transformative potential to meaningful change in my life. I believe a successful day consists of not only thinking about changes you have to make to improve your life, but also of taking action to begin making those changes.

Socrates was famous for many reasons, and is perhaps best known for his statement, "Know thyself." Margaret helped me understand the *self* that I wanted to get to know better, the generous, grateful, "thee and me" *self.*

Thank you, Margaret, for the breakthrough opportunity. I also believe this is the same *self* that Paul, my real estate mentor, referred to when he said he wanted to deal with the optimistic me, not the me that thinks small.

The myth I believed:

Those who get the most toys and attention experience life at its richest.

The reality I discovered:

Those who feel grateful, and are eternally generous, experience life at its richest.

CHAPTER 19

The Maasai Mother

--◈--

The myth I believed:

There is a logical limit to personal power.

As I began my quest to be more open to my authentic nature, the part that thinks in terms of "thee and me," I became curious about how people in other cultures express themselves and relate to each other. I wanted to visit places that were less affected by the vanity and hectic demands of the modern world where money had become God. Africa seemed like a great start.

So I took off for Tanzania where I'd planned a safari on the Serengeti plains. I hired a guide to steer me in the right direction so I could get the most out of a three-week trek. What most interested me was the idea of visiting a remote Maasai village for a week. This appealed to me, because I'd read about the Maasai people, renowned for their strength and integrity. When this part of the trip was finalized, I was wide-eyed and ready for anything to happen.

When the time came to visit the Maasai village, we arrived in a bright red rental Jeep. The villagers went about their business without giving us much attention, and invited us to pitch a tent by the fenced area that protected their cattle from predators.

I was immediately taken by the ease and purposefulness they demonstrated while taking care of their daily chores. There was a conspicuous absence of the drama and senseless theatrics that is often found in the modern world.

One woman, the mother of an infant and a young child about age five, particularly caught my attention. During the day, her child attended a community childcare center while she went about her farming chores with the infant strapped to her chest in a cloth sling. I noticed that she constantly tended to the baby with a sense of urgency. When I got close enough, I could see why—the child was obviously ill. His bloated little belly heaved up and down from labored breathing, and he looked pained and frail.

My heart went out to the baby, and I asked my guide if we should jump in the jeep and find medical care. He told me that we shouldn't interfere; if they wanted our help, they'd ask for it. He went on to explain that the mother would go about her daily chores until the time approached when the infant's life spirit was ready to leave his body. This was the first time that it actually struck me that the baby could be dying. My guide explained to me that the mother would partake in a ritual, unique to this tribe, asking the sun god to take the life-force energy from her baby's body so he would suffer no longer. I was instructed to observe only, from a distance, and do not get involved.

This concept was very new to me, and very difficult to accept. I felt frustrated and helpless—and compelled to keep a vigil of sorts as this tragedy unfolded.

Within a couple of days, flies began gathering around the baby's eyes, which, I was told, was a sign to the mother that the baby's time was near. My guide explained to me that every Maasai village has own way of doing things; and in this village, there would be an evening ritual performed by the chief, blessing the baby's spirit before it passed over to the other side. The next morning the mother would take the baby away from the village and perform another ritual, this one offering the baby's life-force energy up to the sun from whence it came.

That evening, there was a spiritual ritual, with a bonfire, dancing, and chanting. I was told that early the next morning the mother would leave the village with her baby. I was awake pretty much all night, and very early the next morning, from the door of my tent I saw the mother leave her hut with her baby strapped to her chest. She walked next door and left her older child with a neighbor, and she began her trek.

I followed at a respectful distance as she walked about a mile to a meadow where the grass was fairly short. I stood in the meadow, about twenty yards behind her, and waited to see what was going to unfold next. There was something serious, solemn, and very tender about the moment. I felt my heart beating like a muffled drum as I quietly committed to sharing her vigil no matter what might happen next.

For one short instant, I had a sense that this meadow had just become a sacred site, and I'd been given the privilege to be part of something that could well overwhelm me. Slowly, but with no doubt or hesitation, I sat down on the grass and waited.

At the far edge of the meadow, the short grass turned into underbrush leading to the thicket of the jungle. The Maasai mother stood in the center of the meadow, and made a nest of grass. She gently placed the infant in it and sat next to her baby with her hand on his chest, patiently waiting.

As the morning sun began to rise, and night broke into day, the sun rose above the jungle trees. Sunlight moved over the meadow, like fingertips, toward the baby. The mother stood up and stretched her arms outward, palms up, facing the sun. She began chanting in a beautiful voice, "*Sunna wunna yunna, o-wayo wunna, sunna wunna yunna, o-wayo wunna. Sunna wunna yunna, o-wayo wunna, sunna wunna yunna, o-wayo wunna.*" Again and again.

I learned later that the chant was the mother's way of asking the sun god to take the very life-force energy from the baby so the baby would no longer suffer. This tribe's belief was that humans get their animating spirit (life-force energy) from the sun. When they die, that animating spirit returns to its source.

The woman continued to chant, "*Sunna wunna yunna, o-wayo wunna, sunna wunna yunna, o-wayo wunna,*" in a soft and melodious voice.

Within twenty minutes or so, the sun was shining bright on the meadow, and the animal life in the jungle was noisily awakening. Signs of life were everywhere, from the fluttering of birds to the chittering and yowls of different animals. I could also see movement beginning to stir in the brush.

The awakening of the jungle alone was a sight to behold. A large giraffe ambled out of the thicket, looked around, and walked back to the trees to nibble on some leaves. A mother monkey appeared with a baby in tow, chattered, and quickly retreated.

What happened next truly alarmed me. A large male hyena, maybe 140 pounds of solid muscle walked slowly out of the jungle thicket, saliva dripping from his mouth. *Was his appetite whetted by the smell of impending death?* He approached within twenty yards of the woman and her infant and began making a low growling sound.

I braced myself.

Unfazed and without missing a beat, the Maasai mother continued her chant, ignoring the hyena completely. "*Sunna wunna yunna, o-wayo wunna, sunna wunna yunna, o-wayo wunna.*"

At this point, things had gone beyond anything I could have imagined. Even more incredible, the hyena began crawling forward on his belly, making an eerie whining noise, and stopped still.

Did he sense he was part of some grand order of things?

Only a minute or so later, the infant's belly rose and fell . . . one last time. Uncannily, all of the sounds and commotion of the jungle stopped at that very moment.

The mother looked down at her baby, paused for a moment, and kneeled and reached over to touch the baby's belly. She looked up at the sun, looked down again at her baby, picked him up, and kissed him on the forehead. She stood up with the baby in her arms and bowed to the sun.

She then did something I found incomprehensible. She

turned to the hyena, who was now sitting up like a well-trained German Shepherd. She took one step toward him, looked directly at him, and bowed, as if acknowledging his patience.

I could no longer impose on this sacred moment. I quickly and quietly turned and made my way back to the village without glancing back.

Several hours later, I saw the mother, going about her work, but now with her older child by her side. Her face looked sad, yet she carried on with her chores like everyone else in the village. I spent the remaining hours of the day sitting under a tree, pondering the remarkable events that had transpired since the wee hours of the morning.

During the next couple of weeks in Africa, I witnessed nature unedited—beautiful, raw, and brutal. Nothing I saw, however, had nearly as profound an influence on me as the experience of watching the woman who chanted to the sun and kept a hyena at bay. I would never again see the world or humanity the same way.

I realized something important that day in Africa. This Maasai mother demonstrated the biblical statement, "God hath made man upright." When it comes to using your power and directing the universe to work with you, your age doesn't matter, your race doesn't matter, your gender doesn't matter. Your religious indoctrination, your political affiliation, or the level of your education—none of that matters.

This mother was not going to allow any circumstance to discredit the fact that she was made rightly, that she was endowed with all the rich qualities that give dignity to humanity. Her courage, poise, integrity, and her deep conviction to do what she had to do left me in awe, envious of her inner wealth, the kind of wealth that holds infinitely more value than monetary riches.

To this day, when I need a shot of inspiration, I quietly chant, "*Sunna wunna yunna, o-wayo wunna, sunna wunna yunna, o-wayo wunna.*" The very sounds remind me that I am made upright, and that I demonstrate my real power when I act with faith in myself and trust in the natural orderly working of the universe.

I've shared this chant with others numerous times and explained what it means to me, hoping they'd get a sense of who they really are. The power is in the feeling that you get when you chant it, not in the words. Try it. I believe you'll like it. Maybe even love it.

The myth I believed:

There is a logical limit to personal power.

The reality I discovered:

With a conviction to go beyond oneself, personal power is without limit.

CHAPTER 20

License and Registration, Please

The myth I believed:

**It often takes a clever excuse
to get off the hook.**

One day, while doing one of my favorite daily chores—walking to the post office to mail some letters, I heard someone call out "Rob." It was a neighbor of twenty years. Don walked quickly to catch up with me, and we exchanged pleasantries. As we walked together, Don proceeded to tell me that his niece, Carol, was looking for a new place to live because her current apartment was being converted to a condominium, and she was being evicted.

Don knew I owned a building in the location where Carol was hoping to find a small studio and was wondering if I had any vacancies. I told him that my rental broker, Sheila, handled all of my properties. I agreed to give her office a quick call to ask if anything was available. Sheila mentioned that a studio was indeed coming up for grabs and that she about to list it for rent.

I called Don and told him to have his niece call me at the office. I was candid and said that I keep business and friendships separate—I rarely get involved in rentals, and she'd need to qualify like anyone else would. All things being equal, I'd be happy to rent to her.

Carol phoned me within the hour, and we had a delightful chat. I was impressed with her energy and career goals in hotel management, and I encouraged her to fill out an application and get a reference from her landlord. A long pause ensued; I sensed the conversation was about to take an unexpected turn.

"Well, I don't want to waste your time, Mr. White. I was hoping you'd accept me, and we could skip the formalities."

"You mean, like an application, credit check, and a reference from your current landlord?"

"Yes, those kinds of things."

"What's the problem, Carol?" I asked.

This was followed by another pause, this one punctuated with a slight gasp of nervousness, as if she were about to get caught telling a fib.

"Well, my roommates and I always paid our rent. But usually not on time. The landlord won't renew our lease because of the late payments. I'm behind on my student loan payments; and I've let credit card payments slip, too, so I'm sure my credit score isn't looking very good."

I ignored what her uncle had said about the condo conversion—maybe that's what she told him, or maybe he was protecting her. Either way, it was time to get down to brass tacks and ask her why I should choose her as a tenant over someone who had good credit and a good landlord referral. I braced myself for the litany of excuses that I've heard over the years, ranging from, "I was stupid and trusted my boyfriend . . . he'd always borrow money from me and never pay it back, but he's gone now so things are getting better for me," to "It's impossible to make ends meet these days, but I promise I'll always pay my rent before I pay any of my other bills."

What Carol said was not at all what I expected.

"I could come up with a dozen reasons for not having good credit, Mr. White, but the truth is, I simply didn't take responsibility for paying my bills on time, or paying them at all for that matter. I wish I could do it over, because I can see the problems I've caused myself."

I really appreciated her honesty and told her I'd think about it, but I still needed her to fill out an application and get it to my rental agent. Carol thanked me and later that day she made a trip to Sheila's office, making sure to mention our conversation. I also called Sheila to let her know that Carol would be filling out an application for the studio apartment.

The next morning, Sheila called me, curious about why I'd consider such a risky applicant. To be sure, her credit report was marginal at best and the fact that she couldn't get a recommendation from her prior landlord left a gaping hole in her rental application.

"I wouldn't do it, Rob, but you're the boss," Sheila said.

I wrestled with the decision, sometimes going with my head—"Don't do it," and sometimes with my heart—"Give the young woman a chance." I reminded myself about how my disciplined approach to business was critical to my success, and the few times I let other factors override the rules I usually paid a price.

But Carol's honesty was refreshing, and I wanted to reinforce it. Perhaps she'd pass along this lesson to others and be an inspiration for them. The worst case, I made a wrong choice, hoping to help someone who was looking for a break. So I decided to take a leap of faith.

When I called Carol to tell her that the apartment was hers, she was ecstatic. But I still needed to let her know that we always have the choice of taking on one of two roles: the helpless victim who says, "poor me," or the person who takes responsibility. I told her that those who choose "poor me" find themselves whining about life, while those who choose self-responsibility find themselves winning in life.

"I'm breaking a pretty basic rule of good property management," I went on to say, "but I have a feeling that you're ready to choose self-responsibility."

And prove it she did. Carol rented from me for the next two years. During that time, she didn't hit the first of the month more than a few times; the rest of the time her checks arrived a few days early, and she always wrote "Thank you" on the check.

Now, here's the kicker. Just a few hours after I called Carol to tell her the apartment was hers, I was rushing to an appointment and failed to notice a radar trap brilliantly placed in a wide shoulder on the highway. The power balance was reversed, and I was the one facing an authority figure.

Several cars were lined up on the side of the road, as if they were queued up at the take out window of a fast-food restaurant, and now my car was one of them. When the officer got to my car, he looked at me and around the car suspiciously. Satisfied that I wasn't up to anything beyond breaking the speeding law, he asked for my license and registration. He went back to his cruiser to run my license.

A few minutes later, he returned and asked, "Do you know how fast you were going?"

I realized that this was a pivotal moment for me. I was on the razor's edge of choice; which would it be, what role would I choose—"Poor me" or "self-responsibility"? This was the very lesson that I'd given to Carol earlier that day!

I could see he was ready for a stock excuse, just as I was when I asked Carol about her late rent history.

Uh, I had no idea, officer. How fast was I going? Bzzz.

Hmm, my speedometer has been acting up lately—I was just on my way to the repair shop when you stopped me. Bzzzz.

My mother is seriously ill, and I'm rushing over to help her—I was too worried about her to pay attention to the speed. Bzzzzz.

Instead of concocting something or trying to outsmart this seasoned officer, I decided to choose the role of self-responsibility. "Officer, I've just run ten excuses through my head, all lame." I said, "but the fact is, I was going seventyish in a fifty-five zone; almost everyone else was going that fast also, but that doesn't make it legal. I was speeding."

His eyebrows rose, just as mine did when Carol told me why she was a late payer. He looked at me for another five seconds and said, "You're the first one today to simply admit straight out that you were speeding. This time I'm going to give you a warning. Next time it's a ticket. Slow down. Speeding kills."

And with that, I thanked him and continued on my way, the speedometer needle pointing precisely at fifty-five miles per hour or less for the rest of the trip.

Thomas Jefferson said, "Honesty is the first chapter in the book of wisdom." I like to think that I'm becoming a little wiser as I'm growing older. I see moments like the speed trap as life's way of throwing me a pop quiz to see if I'm still growing and if I'm practicing what I'm preaching. Nothing satisfies more than passing such a quiz. It means that I'm walking my talk; I'm living my life according to what's important and true.

The myth I believed:

It often takes a clever excuse to get off the hook.

The reality I discovered:

If I hold myself accountable, no problem is insurmountable—what hook?

CHAPTER 21

I Decided Not to Die

❖

The myth I believed:

Some folks are superior—lucky them.

I still enjoy taking an occasional exotic trip, but most of my traveling these days is on foot around local ponds, arboretums, and mountain paths. I've walked the local seven-mile path around the local pond and down through the wooded trail a thousand times. If the weather is above 65 degrees, Shakespeare (my parrot friend) accompanies me. He sits on my shoulder, letting my legs do the walking while we both do some talking. I've been called his human valet. And I've heard kids ask their parents, when they think they're out of earshot of me, "Is he a pirate?"

Shaky and I both get a kick out of it.

The walking path around the local pond is home to an incredible community, a microcosm of individuals representing all walks of life. During a typical spin around the water's edge, we bump into old people and young people. School teachers and college professors. Municipal workers and doctors. Shop owners and shoppers. Homeless people and wealthy people. That's the pond in a nutshell. And that's one big reason I love it.

One of my favorite pond characters is Peter, a guy in his fifties who sold peanuts at Boston's celebrated Fenway Park for three decades. He's proud of his Fenway vendor days, and it shows in his attitude when he talks about them. One of the keys to Peter's tenure at Fenway was his booming voice; you could hear him from 100 feet away. It was kind of an occupational hazard, though—he was so used to hollering while selling at the stadium that he forgot how to modulate his voice even when he's standing right next to you. I always knew Peter was around the corner after the next corner because he'd bellow, from fifty yards away, "Hey, Bawbby, how's Shake 'n Bake?"

That's what he called Shakespeare, despite my attempts to explain that my feathered companion wasn't anything like a chicken and was no doubt quite insulted by the comparison.

That was all part of the game; Peter got a kick out of the interaction.

I'd often bring up the Fenway Park peanut vending business, knowing that Peter would repeatedly explain the secret of his selling success at Fenway. "You gotta say it like this, Bawbby: 'Get yapeeenuts, heeeeyah!' If you don't say it right, you won't sell peanuts," he insisted.

On the surface, Peter and I lived in two very different worlds. Yet, the pond was a great equalizer; we were just a couple of human beings having a great time enjoying nature's many wonders, like the elegant swans and albino squirrel that live there. Peter would say, "Look at the size of those swans, Bawbby. And they stay so clean and white. How do they do that? And then there's Snow White" [that's the name I'd given the squirrel, since I'd secretly adopted her]. He didn't say this once; he said it every time our paths crossed and a swan was present, which was fairly often.

I'd grown fond of Peter, and was pretty startled one day when I spotted him walking slowly and in a debilitated way. I hadn't seen him for about five months and assumed that our schedules had been out of sync. As soon as we were within eyeshot, I saw that schedules weren't the issue. He looked terrible. His face and hands were puffy and swollen, his breathing labored, and his skin sallow and sagging. The bounce that propelled him around Fenway Park for years had given way to a plodding shuffle. Most alarming, he was bent over as if he'd suddenly aged thirty years.

"Hey, Peter, what's going on?" I asked.

"Bawbby, I'm dying!" he exclaimed with a scratchy, weakened voice. "Doctor says my liver and kidneys are bad."

After an awkward pause, I said, "Well, I'm sorry to hear that."

"I'm sorry, too," Peter said. "And I'm sorry for calling Shakespeare Shake 'n Bake."

"That's okay. Shaky will forgive you," I said, although I knew the bird had a long memory for insults.

Over the next couple of months when we met, I could see that Peter had declined significantly. His fingers were more swollen that before, and his eyes had sunken into his pasty face. He moved at a fraction of his normal speed. Most concerning, he didn't have anything to say.

"Jeez, Peter. I hope you're taking care of yourself," I'd say.

"Well, Bawbby, you know I'm dying."

Then I stopped seeing Peter. After many months, I asked others in the pond community if they'd heard anything more about Peter. Marie, who owns a local bakery, said, "There's been no sighting of Peter for a good six months. I thought the worst . . ."

I nodded to Marie, and we continued our respective walks. As I finished the loop, I figured I'd seen Peter for the last time. I contemplated the impact of his loss on the pond ecosystem—our lives were all interconnected and interdependent on so many subtle levels.

About a year after I met Marie, I was halfway through a solo pond walk (too cold for Shaky) and the equivalent of a sonic boom reverberated across the pond, "Hey, Bawbby, where's Shake 'n Bake?"

I rubbed my eyes, because there was Peter. This sure wasn't the Peter I would have expected to encounter, at least not in this lifetime. No, this was the old Peter, restored to his vibrant, gregarious self. The swelling was gone, and his color looked good. He moved with the determination and grace of a seasoned peanut seller bounding his way through the bleachers.

"Peter, you look incredible!" I gasped. "What happened?"

"I decided not to die."

"You *what?*"

"I woke up a couple of months ago and decided not to die, Bawbby."

"Tell me more."

"I went to the doctor and told him, 'You know what? I'm going to take that medicine, and I'm going to eat what you want me to eat. I'm going to start exercising. You know why, Doc? I've decided not to die.'"

"Peter, this is a miracle," I said.

"No, it's not, Bawbby. I just decided not to die." He paused and said, "I'll catch you on the rebound."

Peter had introduced this phrase to the pond walkers. "Catch you on the rebound" meant "I'll catch up with you again on the second lap around." All the regulars said it to one another, and laughed.

I gave Peter a pat on the back and continued my first lap, musing about how this ex-peanut vendor had developed incredible faith in himself as a self-healer, as much as anyone I've read about. I was certain of one thing: As long as Peter was committed to catching life on the rebound again and again, he'll be in it for the whole ball game.

A week went by, and I couldn't get Peter out of mind. One day at the pond, thinking about Peter's deep conviction to get well, Shakespeare and I came face to face with our resident pond philosopher, a homeless guy we called Swami Charles. This guy has enough pearls of wisdom to choke a jumbo oyster. After saying good morning, I decided to take a cue from conversations I had with Peter. I commented on how lovely and elegant the swans looked.

"As do the pigeons," Swami Charles responded. "Nature makes nothing but first class. Look at the beauty in a dandelion, and you'll stop calling it a weed. All life has incredible purpose, or it wouldn't exist. There are no weeds, just beautiful flowers; no mongrels, just purebred pups, no ugly ducklings, just beautiful swans in many different forms.

Swami Charles explained that only human beings are so foolish as to demote themselves to second class or even third-class status, and demote beautiful, yellow dandelions to weed status. "We're all part of the infinite, which is infinitely perfect."

With that, he went on to say that we make important decisions every day; and if we make them, knowing that we're first class in the eyes of the Creator, we'll live long and laugh a lot.

As I continued my walk, I thought about Peter. I believe that at some point over the previous year, Peter accepted the fact that he was *first class* in every way. And so he decided to live longer and laugh a lot more. Do you accept the fact that you're first class?

The myth I believed:

Some folks are superior—lucky them.

The reality I discovered:

We're all superior—lucky us.

EPILOGUE

Planet Earth offers us life in ultra high definition. When we're born, we're given a pass to the front row of the stage of life. From this vantage point, we get to meet with unexpected gurus who inspire us to raise the bar higher on our own goals and aspirations.

Most of us think of someone else when we learn a life lesson or come to a new understanding about how to win at life. If we're not asking, "What's this got to do with my growth and development?" we're not using our pass to get up front and close to life; we're sitting in the back row seats. Use your pass; dare to ask!

If you're sitting in the back, it's time to make a move. The show is still going on. It's a great show. It's your show! Step up front; step into your power; stop watching life as a distant spectator. Nothing's holding you back except you. Open your eyes to what life is trying to show you.

There is so much more in life that is for you than against you. Life is always urging you onward and upward. With deeper self-understanding comes new self-evaluation. And then comes self-determination to act on what you learn. It takes more energy to resist life than it does to embrace it. Use your energy productively, and you become your own good fortune at every turn.

I promise that when you begin living your life from awareness of the hidden teachers in your midst, you'll find yourself living with a new kind of curiosity, one that has you looking at life through the lens of transformational opportunities. Who knows? Perhaps you'll get an autograph from an unexpected guru or two!

Go to www.robwhitemedia.com to get your free pass to the front row of your life.

ACKNOWLEDGMENTS

My sister Buffy, who left this world as I was finishing this book, was a major source of inspiration throughout my life. She got me through many trying moments when I was growing up. As an adult, she never looked at me through the eyes of my past history; she always saw me, in each moment, as pure potentiality. She continually reminded me that my future was unlimited, even when I saw boundaries and barriers. Buffy taught me to avoid people who say, "I couldn't" or "I wouldn't" succeed. She was an embodiment of generosity, and this book is first and foremost a tribute to her.

While Buffy was the underlying motivation for writing this book, many other precious friends were instrumental in helping to make the work a reality. My friend Steve asked me a thousand questions about my life; many of the answers led to the contents of this book. Steve relentlessly asked and asked, probing deeper—always helping me to clarify what I was trying to convey. Thanks, buddy! And thanks to Ruth and Audrey for looking over Steve's shoulder to help with the editing.

Thank you, Nick, for being one of the unexpected gurus in my life. Although, you're not mentioned in any of the stories, you've been a ready ear for the past several years when I shared my insights. These conversations helped me refine my ideas so I could offer them to the world, hopefully helping others to understand themselves better.

Thank you, Marly, for your excellent final edit of the book, bringing more focus to the messages.

A special thanks goes to Shakespeare, my fine-feathered companion of thirty years. A bright green-and-yellow Amazon parrot, Shakespeare (aka "Shaky"), took many long walks around our local pond with me and patiently listened while I spoke of the key concepts I wanted to share in this book. He's not only a great listener, but he taught me that a noisy mind causes confusion, and that in silence we find answers. Now that this book is complete, I'll make it up to you in extra almonds, Shaky—I'm buying.

Final thanks go to my wife Kat. I learn a lot more from a gentle "No" from Kat than a thousand thoughtless "Yeses" from the world. Thank you for teaching me.

ABOUT THE AUTHOR

Rob White is a philosopher, story teller, author, and inspirational speaker. He's also a pretty funny guy to listen to. Rob inspires folks to look at their lives through the lens of transformational opportunities so they can come back home to their naturally curious and ambitious nature.

Rob was dissatisfied with his life, and inspired to do something about it. His "inspirational dissatisfaction" was the catalyst that took Rob from a mill town kid destined to work in a local factory, to a teaching career in a major city, to being a highly successful real estate developer and restaurateur with holdings in Massachusetts and California. Most recently, he became an essayist and book author. With determination and passion, over and over again, Rob reinvented himself.

Rob currently enjoys homes on the East and West coasts, spending much of his time writing in Boston. He gets great delight teaching classes on the "Wow Factor" at Northeastern University.

Rob believes that the most practical lesson he can teach his students, one that opens them to an entirely new kind of happiness that assures a very bright future, is this: when you do your work, *seek excellence* above all else, and *always* do the best you can." Rob is convinced that people who follow this two-step formula will not only repeatedly find themselves doing better, but will find that it gets easier to achieve their dreams. And that's because, as Rob is often heard saying, "The easier it gets, the easier it gets."

Learn more at www.robwhitemedia.com.